LOST CHICAGO
DEPARTMENT STORES

Leslie Goddard

THE
History
PRESS

Published by The History Press
Charleston, SC
www.historypress.com

Front cover, top left: AP photo; top center: LC-D4-34699/Library of Congress/ Prints and Photographs Division; top right: DN-A-4841/*Chicago Sun-Times/ Chicago Daily News* Collection/Chicago History Museum; bottom: UPI Newspictures.
Back cover: HB-11306-B3/Chicago History Museum/Hedrich-Blessing Collection; insert: HB-07810-F/Chicago History Museum/Hedrich-Blessing Collection.

Unless otherwise noted, all images are courtesy of the author.

First published 2022

Manufactured in the United States

ISBN 9781467147712

Library of Congress Control Number: 2021950615

CONTENTS

Acknowledgements 5

Introduction 7

1. Marshall Field's: Give the Lady What She Wants 19
2. Carson Pirie Scott: Carson's Is for Me 39
3. The Fair: Everything for Everybody Under One Roof 56
4. Montgomery Ward: Satisfaction Guaranteed or
    Your Money Back 61
5. Goldblatt's: The Incredible Bargain Centers 74
6. Wieboldt's: Where You Buy with Confidence 87
7. Sears, Roebuck: Cheapest Supply House on Earth 99
8. The Competition: Specialty and Neighborhood
    Department Stores 116
9. Christmas on State Street 133

Epilogue 147
Notes 157
Index 171
About the Author 176

ACKNOWLEDGEMENTS

Every time I give a lecture on the history of Chicago's department stores, I am struck by how enthusiastic audiences become. People clamor to tell me stories of going to State Street with their grandmother or aunt or mother, wearing white gloves and hats. They reminisce about eating in the Walnut Room at Marshall Field's, visiting the S&H Green Stamps redemption center at Wieboldt's and riding the kiddie monorail at Sears. More than anything, they remember the Christmas window displays and how it felt to walk from one department store to the next, braced against the December wind and loving the magical excitement of it.

My family has similar memories. My maternal grandmother loved The Fair, with its friendly, approachable atmosphere and great prices. My paternal grandmother's preferred store was Marshall Field's. From her, I inherited an exquisite Field's embroidered tablecloth—and a love for the Field's Special Sandwich (iceberg lettuce, turkey, Swiss cheese and bacon, smothered in Thousand Island dressing). Years later, my mother began an annual tradition (common to many Chicago families) of bringing her granddaughters to the Walnut Room in December to eat under the great Christmas tree. We always ordered chicken pot pie and ended the meal with a slice of Frango mint ice cream pie.

My family even has some employee connections to these stores. My grandfather worked for Marshall Field's for twenty-six years, serving at various times as merchandise manager for children's wear and toys, buyer for linens and manager of the Far Eastern buying office in Tokyo, Japan.

He later joined Carson Pirie Scott, and my mother sometimes took me and my sister downtown to see him in his office in that awe-inspiring building at State and Madison Streets. My father-in-law worked at Montgomery Ward for many years, as did my stepmother, who fondly remembers her coworkers as one big family.

This book would not have been possible without memories like these, from shoppers and employees alike. Memories are the heart of what made these stores worth remembering. I appreciate everyone who took the time to share their wonderful, funny, nostalgic and often poignant memories with me. I also send warm appreciation to every Chicago newspaper reporter and magazine writer who took the time over the years to collect and preserve stories about these department stores, especially those stores that disappeared long ago.

There are many others to thank as well. A huge thank-you goes to the staff at the Chicago History Museum for access to its wonderful *Chicago Sun-Times*, *Chicago Daily News* and Hedrich-Blessing photographic archives. For additional help with photographs, deep appreciation goes to Megan Klintworth, Abraham Lincoln Presidential Library; Ann Panthen, Champaign County Historical Archives, Urbana Free Library; Brittan Nannenga, DePaul University; Tony Dudek, Tribune Content Agency; and Allyson Smally, Sulzer Regional Library, Chicago Public Library. Special thanks to Ben Gibson and Rick Delaney at The History Press for their help, enthusiasm and patient advice, especially when the COVID-19 pandemic upset the initial research plans for this book.

Finally, thank you to my mother, who provided endless advice and patient feedback at every step of the process. And to Bruce, who has never enjoyed shopping but loves listening to stories about department stores.

INTRODUCTION

In 1947, the *Chicago Tribune* declared State Street "the world's greatest shopping center." Altogether, it said, stores along the city's famous downtown retail corridor had more than one thousand acres of sales space, making it the greatest concentration of shopping in the world.[1] State Street's stores served 450,000 customers daily, with sales adding up to more than $400 million annually.[2] You could purchase anything on State Street, it said, from a needle to an airplane.

Seven department stores dominated the market: Sears, Roebuck and Company; Goldblatt Brothers; The Fair; Carson Pirie Scott and Company; The Boston Store; Mandel Brothers; and, highest of all in reputation, Marshall Field and Company. Two others—Montgomery Ward and Company and Wieboldt's Stores—did not yet have a State Street presence but soon would.

It was a startling change from one hundred years earlier. In the 1840s, Chicago's first small retail corridor had centered on Lake Street, close to the Chicago River and convenient to the city's prominent shipping industry.

Potter Palmer, more than any other merchandising visionary, saw the potential in a muddy, boisterous young Chicago when he opened a dry-goods firm in 1852 at 137 Lake Street.[3] After building it into a successful wholesale and retail operation, he sold the business to his partners (Marshall Field and Levi Leiter) and turned his attention to real estate. Beginning in the mid-1860s, he bought properties along State Street, with an eye to pivoting Chicago's commercial axis from Lake to State Street. Whereas

Locations of Chicago's major department stores on State Street in 1947 (not to scale).
Wieboldt's and Montgomery Ward existed in 1947, but neither had a store on State Street yet.

Lake Street was hemmed in by the river and by railroads, State Street offered space to expand. It also had some of Chicago's earliest tracks for horse-drawn streetcars.

To anchor his new commercial district at one end, he built a lavish hotel, the eponymously named Palmer House at State and Monroe Streets. At the other end, he put up a marble structure at State and Washington Streets and convinced Field and Leiter to move their dry-goods business there, which they did in 1868. State Street rapidly surpassed Lake Street as Chicago's preferred shopping district.

The Great Chicago Fire destroyed much of this work but laid the foundation for the rise of a new type of city shopping that accompanied Chicago's reemergence from the fire. In 1873—when Ernst J. Lehmann opened a store called The Fair at State and Adams Streets—only a few dozen department stores existed in the entire United States. By 1900, there were more than one thousand.

Chicago, more than any other American city, embraced the department store, leading the way in the marriage of merchandising and architecture that would become distinctive for department stores. "In no other city has the department store gained the same hold on the people as it has in Chicago," said the *Arena* in 1897, declaring that "Chicago department stores are larger, more numerous, and transact more business than do those of any of the eastern cities."[4]

What led Chicago department stores to become bigger, busier and more competitive than those anywhere else in the country? For one thing, Chicago had the perfect conditions for this new type of retail, especially in its embrace of new forms of urban transportation. Public transportation nurtured department stores, carrying passengers right into the core of the city's commercial district.[5] Chicago had horse-drawn streetcars by 1859, a cable car system by 1882 and elevated trains beginning in 1897.[6] By that time, central Chicago already had the nickname "the Loop."

Chicago's great department store magnates also benefited from the availability of large infusions of capital, often coming from industrialists and real estate speculators.[7] Abram Rothschild entered the department store business after marrying into the family of Nelson Morris, one of Chicago's legendary meat-packers. Levi Leiter, after splitting from his longtime partner Marshall Field, went into real estate. In 1891, he hired architect William Le Baron Jenney to build a fireproof structure that would become known as the Second Leiter Building. The department store Siegel, Cooper leased the building, whose innovative structural engineering permitted wide-open expanses of floor space (the building later became the downtown flagship of Sears).

As it expanded in population and wealth, Chicago attracted ambitious, energetic merchants. None rose higher in reputation than Marshall Field. He began, like so many merchant princes, as a clerk in a dry-goods store, selling various fabrics and fabric items. As he gained knowledge of the textile field and experience in sales, he moved up from clerk to junior partner to full partner. By the 1880s, he and his partner Levi Leiter had built their company, Field, Leiter and Company, into the most prominent wholesale and retail dry-goods firm in Chicago. "When the public goes abroad, it boasts of Field, Leiter and Co. just as it does of the Stock-Yard," read one newspaper editorial.[8]

Over time, like many other dry-goods businesses, Marshall Field's store began adding new departments, such as books, fine china and bric-a-brac that were not traditional to dry-goods stores. By the time Marshall Field's opened an imposing new building at Randolph and State Streets in 1902, it had evolved into a full-line department store, handling everything from furniture and cookware to petticoats and hosiery.

Marshall Field's not only typified the growth of a dry-goods firm into a department store but also typified the emergence of the massive department store building. Here again, Chicago led the way, as one bigger and grander building after another arose. Starting in the 1890s, store after store grabbed the title of "world's largest."[9] First, Siegel, Cooper moved into the Second Leiter Building, with its acres of open, airy floor space in 1891. Then, The Fair completed construction of a modern twelve-story building at State and Adams Streets in 1897. Soon, Schlesinger & Mayer had a new building. Then Mandel Brothers opened its location. Marshall Field's attempted to outdo them, gradually constructing a building that would occupy an entire city block by 1914.

More than 150,000 visitors toured Marshall Field's during the grand-opening celebration of its new 1907 building. They marveled at the building's impressive main floor with its marble flooring, hand-carved mahogany counters and spacious, high ceilings. Massive interior columns stretched the entire 385-foot length of the main aisle, causing one enthusiastic employee to dub it the "cathedral of all the stores."[10]

Towering over the streetcars and pedestrians on State Street, the great department stores rivaled the monumental art museums and civic buildings springing up around the country at the same time. Architect Daniel Burnham of Chicago, who oversaw construction of the Marshall

Pedestrians jam the sidewalk in front of The Boston Store (*left, with clock*) at State and Madison Streets, 1924. Mandel Brothers is visible on the right, and Marshall Field's is in the center distance. *DN-0077873/*Chicago Daily News *collection/Chicago History Museum.*

Field's State Street store, would become the era's most prolific architect of mammoth department store structures. Many Chicago department stores featured extravagant artistic flourishes, like the Louis Comfort Tiffany glass mosaic inside Marshall Field's south rotunda and Louis Sullivan's graceful ornamental ironwork on the façade of Schlesinger & Mayer (later Carson, Pirie, Scott). Giant clocks at both Marshall Field's and The Boston Store functioned almost as sculpture.

Many of these buildings jammed together on State Street, drawing thousands of daily shoppers to the area. By 1897, the department stores on State Street (there were then eight of them) did 90 percent of the city's retail business.[11]

Chicago department stores required large staffs and became some of the city's biggest employers. By 1904, Marshall Field's employed nearly ten thousand people during peak shopping periods.[12] Unlike earlier dry-goods stores, whose clerks were expected to have extensive knowledge of textiles and provide detailed guidance on purchases, the big stores relied more heavily on advertising and visual displays to sell their merchandise. As the need for skilled sales clerks declined, women now came to dominate many retail sales positions. Some store executives defended their decision to hire women, saying female clerks made it easier for female shoppers to converse about fashion trends and get accurate fittings. Others pointed out that women could be hired for these deskilled retail jobs at wages much lower than for men.

Not surprisingly, small- and medium-sized merchants whose business suffered from the rise of the big stores blasted department stores as monopolies. They accused the big stores of using deceitful advertising and unfair labor practices to drive their competitors out of business. When their efforts to rally Chicago shoppers to shun the new emporia drew little support, the small retailers introduced a bill to the Illinois legislature in 1897 forbidding merchants from selling from more than one category of merchandise. If a store sold clothing, hats and caps, for example, it could not also sell furniture and carpets. Hardware and crockery could be sold from the same store, but not bicycles and vehicles. That bill failed, but lawmakers successfully passed a law forbidding fraudulent advertising.[13]

Still, even small retailers benefited from the mushrooming city of the late nineteenth and early twentieth centuries. State Street dominated Chicago's retail business, but the city also had bustling retail districts in outlying areas. Numerous neighborhood shopping districts popped up, often in locations where major streets intersected or around transit transfer points. Many of these neighborhood shopping areas catered to one or more ethnic populations. Here, too, pioneering Chicago department stores emerged. Wieboldt's and Goldblatt's grew into large enterprises by catering to immigrant and working-class shoppers who were not wedded to shopping on State Street.[14] By the 1930s, the South Side had a flourishing commercial area along Forty-Seventh Street serving the city's expanding African American population.

At the same time that some Chicago merchants were revolutionizing brick-and-mortar shopping, other retailers were pioneering mail order. Aaron Montgomery Ward put out his first mail-order catalog in 1872. It consisted of one sheet, listing fabric, glassware and notions. Within two decades, the Montgomery Ward catalog would balloon to more than one thousand pages with a circulation of 730,000. It was soon joined by Richard Sears's general merchandise catalog, launched in 1893. By 1900, according to historian William Leach, nearly 1,200 mail-order companies existed.

Many of them called Chicago home, including two other big catalog firms: the Chicago Mail-Order Company (founded in 1889, later known as Aldens Inc.) and Spiegel (founded in 1865; it issued its first mail-order catalog in 1905). Some, including Aldens and Spiegel, opened retail department stores at least temporarily.

Mail-order catalogs hit their peak popularity from the 1890s through the 1910s, when they transformed how people shopped in the United States, freeing rural Americans from being limited to whatever their local country store stocked. Mail-order catalogs became wish lists for Americans who learned of new trends in clothing, furniture and household appliances through them—and could have items delivered within days. The catalogs also transformed retail, using centralized buying, high turnover and modern accounting to maximize profitability. Mail-order houses passed on those savings to customers, offering merchandise at prices well below those of independent retailers.

Expanding railroads played a crucial role in this expansion of merchandising, enabling quick movement of goods between manufacturers, retailers and consumers. Chicago's department stores and mail-order catalogs used the enormous economies of speed and scale that railroad networks made possible. As the hub of the nation's burgeoning railroad network, Chicago merchants could move goods faster and at lower costs than ever before.

Railroads, however, were only the tip of the technological iceberg. Chicago department stores made pioneering use of new approaches to merchandising and displays that transformed shopping into entertainment. Unlike the drab interiors of dry-goods stores, department stores exploded with color, from mahogany counters to marble floors. Cheaper plate-glass manufacturing methods by the mid-1890s permitted larger, stronger display windows, which soon became standard at the big department stores. Windows became magical stages where display artists presented enticing goods to pedestrians. It had a democratizing impact; even customers who never patronized a particular store might enjoy its displays.

Chicago department stores also embraced the kind of pampering customer services that encouraged shoppers to make all-day visits to their emporia. Plush waiting rooms, tearooms and grills, reading rooms, first-aid stations, children's nurseries, post office stations and ticket agencies abounded. As early as the turn of the twentieth century, department stores featured entertainment and musical performances. Both Carson Pirie Scott and Marshall Field's had choral societies that performed both in-store and

Marshall Field's storefront, with display windows and the clock at State and Randolph Streets visible, 1948. *HB-11306-B3/Chicago History Museum/Hedrich-Blessing Collection.*

at Chicago's Orchestra Hall. The big stores decorated their main aisles and draped their exterior façades for major national occasions.

During the Great Depression, some of the expansive growth of Chicago's top-tier department stores slowed, although the Century of Progress International Exposition from 1933 to 1934 temporarily insulated some city businesses from the worst effects of the financial crisis. But the economic hard times provided opportunities for Chicago's growing discount department stores. Sears opened a huge store on State Street in 1932, its first location in a downtown shopping district. Goldblatt's opened its flagship State Street store in 1936.

By World War II, Chicago's department stores could be justly proud of their national reputation as some of the biggest and best stores in the nation. And Chicago-area shoppers loved them. When the Japanese bombed Pearl Harbor in December 1941, one Chicago woman cried, "Everything is gone! Except, thank goodness, Marshall Field's."[15] After the war, many Chicago department stores moved quickly, modernizing and expanding their stores to accommodate consumers eager to catch up on their unmet needs.

The busy crossroads at Madison and State Streets at midcentury. *Fred Kosth/Archive Photos/ Getty Images.*

As the nation entered the middle of the twentieth century, however, department stores were struggling to retain their position at the vanguard of retail. The biggest challenge was how to appeal to a youthful market. Many of them increased their bridal offerings dramatically at midcentury to capture a younger market, including Marshall Field's, which had opened a bridal secretary office in the 1920s. Carson Pirie Scott estimated that it served five thousand brides in 1948.[16] Most of the big stores had advisory groups of college students to review and approve teen fashions. In 1946, *Life* magazine featured Carson Pirie Scott's college board members, strengthening Carson's reputation for youthful fashionability.[17]

Moreover, the costs of doing business kept rising, even as department stores' share of the retail market kept shrinking. And the struggle only increased as discount stores exploded in numbers in the 1960s. Stores such as Shoppers World, E.J. Korvette and Kmart had a large presence in the Chicago region by the mid-1960s.

Shopping-center branches seemed to be the future of department stores. Some department stores had opened branch locations in outlying commuter suburbs in the 1920s, especially in Oak Park and Evanston, which already had busy retail corridors. Now, they began opening branches as anchors in newly built shopping complexes. The rise of shopping centers began in the Chicago region with projects such as Park Forest Plaza (1949), Old Orchard Center in Skokie (1956) and the Hillside Shopping Center (1956).

Still, customers had strong emotional attachments to the downtown stores, and events such as fashion shows and holiday promotions kept the stores busy. The State Street Council, first organized in 1929, staged promotional events designed to lure Chicagoans to the district. Especially popular was the annual Christmas parade that kicked off the holiday shopping season on State Street every year.

Aerial view of Woodfield Mall in Schaumburg, 1973. Marshall Field's can be seen on the right and Sears on the left. *HB-36950-B1/Chicago History Museum/Hedrich-Blessing Collection.*

However, by the 1970s, Chicagoans mostly went to malls when they wanted to shop the department stores. Regional malls such as Woodfield Mall in Schaumburg, which opened in 1971, attracted shoppers from a broad swath of territory. Within the city, developers responded to the popularity of malls by putting up enclosed shopping complexes such as Ford City (1965) and the Brickyard (1977). Although individual branches of the large department stores did less business than the big downtown stores, taken as a whole, they did much more.[18]

Chicago's State Street department stores looked increasingly threadbare and desolate by this era. The shift in upscale shopping to Michigan Avenue, which had begun in the 1920s after the opening of the Michigan Avenue bridge, accelerated. The seventy-four-story Water Tower Place, opened in 1975, reestablished Chicago as a retail vanguard. Anchored by two department stores, Water Tower Place also featured restaurants, specialty stores, theaters, offices, condominiums and even a hotel.

Chicago's department stores began disappearing from the landscape in large numbers in the 1980s. Today, most of them are gone. But their remarkable legacy lives on. They played a key role in transforming shopping from an errand into a popular pastime—and helped Chicago transform from a pioneer outpost to one of America's great cities.

1.

MARSHALL FIELD'S

Give the Lady What She Wants

In 1952, Marshall Field and Company kicked off its one hundredth anniversary celebration with a lavish party in the Walnut Room restaurant. A twenty-two-foot-high birthday cake sat atop the room's fountain. It bore 101 candles, one for each year plus one to light the way to the future. Distinguished guests enjoyed a fashion show highlighting clothing trends from the 1850s to the 1950s, followed by dinner and dancing. Descendants of old Chicago families shared memories of shopping at "Field's." One guest could even remember opening his store charge account sixty years earlier.[19]

Everything about Marshall Field's in 1952 was grand. Now the second-largest department store in the nation, it served 140,000 customers on an average day and handled 35,000 phone calls. Marshall Field's reportedly imported the largest collection of European designs of any American store. It sold more children's toys than any store in the nation. It was possibly the largest single bookseller in the nation, too.[20]

Even the store's building was massive. In 1914, the store's thirteen-floor structure had grown to encompass an entire city block with more than thirty-five acres of floor space. Its basement budget floor was said to be the largest selling floor with the longest retail aisle in the world. The store's five restaurants on the seventh floor could serve fourteen thousand customers in a single day. No Chicago department store was grander—or more beloved.

It must have surpassed even the wildest dreams of Marshall Field himself. Back in 1856, when the twenty-two-year-old Field arrived in the city,

Left: Marshall Field's executives toast the company's one-hundredth birthday in the Walnut Room, 1952. *Ralph Crane/The LIFE Picture Collection/Shutterstock.*

Opposite: A stereoscope view of the Field, Leiter building at State and Washington Streets, prior to the 1871 Great Chicago Fire.

Chicago was still a frontier town. Although hungry and energetic, the city consisted mostly of muddy streets and wood buildings. Shopping in Chicago was anything but leisurely. Clerks assailed shoppers on entry, regularly misrepresented goods and haggled over prices. A shopping outing required stamina and determination.

Not all merchants approved of that approach. Potter Palmer based his dry-goods store on the principle that treating customers well could pay off. When Palmer opened his six-story P. Palmer Dry Goods store on Lake Street in 1852, he put quality and customer service first. He eliminated haggling and posted prices on the merchandise. He stocked his store with luxury goods as well as everyday basics. Starting in 1861, he announced that he would accept returns for any reason, a startlingly innovative concept for Chicago at the time. P. Palmer Dry Goods soon became the preferred store for Chicago's emerging upper and middle class.

By 1865, however, Palmer was restless and eager to go abroad for his health. He approached two young men, Marshall Field and Levi Z. Leiter, to join him as partners. Both worked at one of Palmer's competitors. Marshall Field, born on a farm in Conway, Massachusetts, in 1834, had distinguished himself as a salesman since arriving in Chicago. He regularly put in twelve-hour days and showed an uncanny knack for anticipating customer needs. Field's talent for salesmanship meshed well with Leiter's deft handling of finances and credit. The firm operated as Field, Palmer and Leiter until 1867, when Palmer left the partnership and it was reorganized as Field, Leiter and Co.

By 1868, Palmer had returned to Chicago and turned his attention to real estate. He convinced Field and Leiter that year to move their business to a lavish new marble-fronted building at State and Washington Streets. The cream of Chicago society arrived for the grand opening of the new "dry goods store in a marble palace."[21] Both partners personally greeted customers at the front door, bestowing a cigar on each man and a rose on each woman. Recognizing Chicagoans' keen interest in imported goods, Marshall Field sent his brother Joseph to Manchester, England, in 1871, to open Field, Leiter and Co.'s first foreign office.[22] By 1900, Field's would have buying offices in Germany, Belgium, France and Japan.

Beginning on the evening of October 8, 1871, the Great Chicago Fire swept through the city. Field and Leiter, along with legions of employees and helpers, scrambled to remove some of the store's costliest merchandise. Wagons loaded with expensive silks and velvets, fine laces, shawls and rugs raced from the burning downtown. Workers draped wet blankets on the roof, trying to save the structure until it became apparent that the building was doomed. Early the next morning, the flames reached Field and Leiter's store. In less than an hour, nothing remained but smoldering ruins.

The two merchants moved quickly. Within three weeks, they had reopened in a converted streetcar barn at State and Twentieth Streets, outside the burnt district. And in October 1873, they were back at State and Washington Streets in an even grander, Italianate-style building. But disaster struck again in 1877, when another fire consumed that building. Undaunted, Field and Leiter again found temporary quarters, this time on Michigan Boulevard (as it was then known). And in 1879, the store again returned to State and Washington Streets, in a building that was its grandest yet.

The relationship between Marshall Field and Levi Leiter frayed, however, as Leiter's brusque personality and partiality for wholesale butted up against Field's preference for retail and attentive customer rapport. Leiter accepted a buyout in 1881, and the firm quietly reorganized as Marshall Field and Company.

Now firmly in command, the forty-seven-year-old Marshall Field used his keen merchandising sense to strengthen his company's reputation as Chicago's finest. He instructed his staff to emphasize the excellence of the merchandise but always accept returns graciously. All customers, he insisted, should be treated with the same courtesy, regardless of their means.

Field's legendary customer service can be summed up in a frequently repeated story about the day he overheard an assistant retail manager exchanging words with a female customer. Field walked over and asked, "What are you doing here?" The manager replied, "I'm settling a complaint." "No, you're not," Field retorted. "Give the lady what she wants."[23] It became the store's mantra and the title of a 1952 book by Lloyd Wendt and Herman Kogan.

Field had a flair for recognizing talented employees, most notably the energetic and imaginative Harry G. Selfridge, who became head of retail operations in 1887. Selfridge pushed through new approaches, installing brighter electric lighting and modern displays that let customers inspect merchandise without the aid of a clerk. He converted the store's basement into a large section for selling budget-priced merchandise, later named the Budget Floor. For Chicago's 1893 World's Columbian Exposition, Selfridge festooned the store with yards of red-white-and-blue bunting, increased the stock of imported goods and spearheaded a new addition, at Wabash Avenue and Washington Street.

Marshall Field (date unknown). *LC-B2-176-15/ Library of Congress/Prints and Photographs Division.*

More than any other single person, Selfridge transformed Marshall Field's from a dry-goods business into a full-fledged department store. In 1884, the store had forty-two sections. By 1898, there were seventy-four. By 1904, the year Selfridge sold his shares in the company, there were more than one hundred.[24]

Still, for all of Selfridge's innovations, Marshall Field's remained an essentially conservative institution. The store shunned the low-brow term *department*, preferring to call the store's departments "sections." For years, executives covered the store's windows on Sundays and refused to advertise in Sunday newspapers. (Years later, in the 1960s, it would be the last major holdout against Sunday hours). Marshall Field even originally rejected Harry Selfridge's idea of an in-store restaurant. The Fair, just down the street, already served food, and Selfridge believed Field's should have even better food service. When Selfridge finally persuaded Field to allow him to open a small tearoom in 1890, it proved an instant success. On the first day, fifty-six diners ate from a menu that included corned beef hash, chicken pot pie, chicken salad, orange punch in an orange shell and Field's rose punch (ice cream with dressing served with a red rose).[25] The store's restaurant space grew steadily larger; by 1903, Field's was serving three thousand diners daily. By the 1920s, virtually the entire seventh floor was given over to tearooms and grills.

For shoppers, an ocean of difference separated Field's from the humbler stores farther south on State Street. Field's put more emphasis on the quality of its merchandise. It provided more services and served more credit customers. When a new building at State and Washington Streets opened in 1902, it included "rooms for checking packages and clothes, a library with Oriental rugs and green leather mahogany furniture, restrooms with green willow rockers, a first-aid room with a trained nurse, and an information bureau that helped settle any difficulties—from getting theater tickets to finding a hotel room."[26] Employees had their own restaurant, recreation rooms, gymnasium, locker rooms with showers and library.

Then, on January 16, 1906, tragedy struck when seventy-one-year-old Marshall Field unexpectedly died, having developed pneumonia after playing a round of golf of New Year's Day in the snow. The store immediately closed for three days of mourning.

John G. Shedd now stepped in as president. He was cut from the same mold as Marshall Field, who had groomed him, and put a strong emphasis on quality merchandise and exceptional customer service. Hired originally as a stock boy, he had worked his way up to head of the company's prosperous wholesale division. Shedd's first major action as president was to move ahead with Field's vision for the building itself. Workers soon demolished the oldest part of the store at State and Washington Streets and put up a new building to match the 1902 structure at State and Randolph Streets. It opened in 1907.

Everything about the new building was massive, speaking to the store's grand presence atop the hierarchy of Chicago department stores. It stood thirteen stories tall, with three subbasements and forty-nine-foot-tall granite columns framing the main entryway on State Street. Architecturally, the structure spoke of solidity and monumentalism, looking more like a bank or government building than a cathedral of shopping.

Two enormous bronze clocks went up, one at State and Washington Streets (replacing an earlier clock installed in 1897) and another at State and Randolph Streets. Each weighed just under eight tons and hung from ornamental ironwork projecting several feet from the building. The face of each clock measured forty-six inches across. Norman Rockwell immortalized the Marshall Field's clocks for the cover of the *Saturday Evening Post* on November 3, 1945, showing a repairman using his modest pocket watch to set one of the magnificent clocks (actually, the clocks are regulated from inside).

More columns stretched along the 385-foot-long main aisle inside the store. Overhead, two grand rotundas soared upward, helping to create an atmosphere of both elegance and beauty. Topping the south rotunda was a

Marshall Field's retail store building, 111 North State Street, circa 1907. *LC-D4-34699/ Library of Congress/Prints and Photographs Division.*

vaulted ceiling with a Louis Comfort Tiffany mosaic made from 1.6 million pieces of iridescent Favrile glass. It took fifty men two years to install it. When the building opened in 1907, so many visitors crowded under the mosaic to view it that Shedd worried the floor might buckle.

The expansive new building allowed Field's to enlarge its services, which by this time included everything from cool-air fur storage to custom interior

Early postcard view of Marshall Field's main aisle showing the Tiffany mosaic vaulted ceiling in the south rotunda.

design. Even in a city where department stores catered to customers' needs, Field's had a reputation for indulging its customers' every desire.

As part of its identity as a high-class store, Field's downplayed its mercenary objectives, preferring to showcase itself as a public servant. Its window displays, created for decades by famed designer Arthur Fraser, often featured only a few select gowns exhibited in an exquisite setting. The store's stylish bimonthly magazine, *Fashions of the Hour* (launched in October 1914), featured articles on society events, interviews with designers and stories about the city's social and cultural events, with store merchandise included almost as an afterthought. It eventually evolved into a more conventional retail catalog, but *Fashions of the Hour* would continue until 1978.

By 1914, the store had expanded along Wabash Avenue all the way to Randolph Street, so that it now occupied an entire city block. That same year, Field's opened a new twenty-one-story building across the street at the southwest corner of Washington Street and Wabash Avenue. The Store for Men occupied the first six floors and three basements, with sales space for men's clothing, shoes, hats, luggage and sports gear, as well as a fifth-floor men's grill with its own Tiffany-glass-domed ceiling.

Shedd also spearheaded a broad expansion of the company's network of mills located across the country to produce such goods as sheets, towels, lace curtains, oriental rugs and even underwear. All were made to Marshall Field's specifications, ensuring they met Field's high standards.

Yet even as its retail sales expanded, Marshall Field's wholesale sales were declining precipitously. Many small-town stores now bought directly from manufacturers, and chain stores had begun replacing mom-and-pop retailers. To shore up its wholesale division, Marshall Field's executives embarked on construction of an enormous new wholesale building that could serve as a consolidated center for many Chicago wholesalers. The Merchandise Mart opened in 1930 as the largest building in the world, but it did little to turn things around. Field's wholesale losses continued to mount. In the mid-1930s, the firm succumbed to the inevitable and began liquidation of its wholesale operations and, eventually, its manufacturing operations as well.

Retail, however, just continued to grow. Anticipating suburban growth, the company began opening branch stores, starting with Lake Forest (1928), Evanston (1929) and Oak Park (1929). The company also acquired the high-end Seattle department store Frederick & Nelson in 1929.

Frederick & Nelson gave Field's one of its icons: the Frango Mint, although the term *Frango* was not originally used for a chocolate-mint

Above: Window display featuring women's dresses at Marshall Field's, circa 1944. *HB-07810-F/Chicago History Museum/Hedrich-Blessing Collection.*

Opposite: Men's hat section on the main floor of Marshall Field's Store for Men, 1946. *HB-09004-E/Chicago History Museum/Hedrich-Blessing Collection.*

candy. The treat debuted in 1918 at Frederick & Nelson as a maple-flavored, frozen, custard-like dessert. The maple Frango began appearing on Marshall Field's restaurant menus in the 1930s. Not until after World War II did the Chicago store begin using the term for chocolate-mint candies called Frango Mints. (Frederick & Nelson had introduced its own Frango Mint candies back in 1928 or 1929.) As Robert Spector has shown, "Contrary to legend, there is no record that Frango Chocolate was ever called 'Francos,' and no basis to the oft-repeated story that the name was changed to Frango Chocolate because animosity towards Spain's Generalissimo Franco caused sales to drag."[27]

Marshall Field's emerged grander than ever after World War II. The downtown store was spruced up with millions of dollars' worth of improvements and modernizations. Marshall Field's remained the pinnacle of elegance, with a reputation for the highest-quality merchandise.

Nothing epitomized that more than the 28 Shop, the company's in-store boutique for couture fashion. Opened in 1941, the section took its name from its private elevator entrance at 28 East Washington Street. The 28 Shop featured high-end fashions from top American designers and then, after the war, international designers as well. A 1950s store guidebook

Left: A 1947 advertisement for Marshall Field's Frango Mints, priced at $1.50 a pound.

Right: A 1942 advertisement for Marshall Field's recently opened 28 Shop.

proudly asserted, "A few weeks after Balenciaga introduces a new jacket line, you'll find it at Field's, adapted for every figure type, every age, every purse."[28]

The 28 Shop, however, was only the most exclusive of Marshall Field's many illustrious sections. Store galleries sold antique silver, antiques and fine art. The eighth-floor furniture section included a model home called the Trend House that showcased trends in interior design. Staff on the sportsmen's floor in the Store for Men could correct your golf swing or suggest the best tackle for tuna fishing. The company's toy department "was easily the best toy store in the city. Half of the fourth floor was devoted exclusively to toys," recalled blogger James Iska. "To this day, the very words, 'The Fourth Floor of Fields' resonate with magic in my ears."[29]

Marshall Field's customer service, always a point of pride, had now become legendary. *Give the Lady What She Wants* tells the story of a woman who brought a pair of button shoes, purchased in 1908, to the shoe department in 1946. She had broken her ankle soon after buying them, put them away and forgot about them. She presented the receipt and received a full refund of her $2.97.[30]

Well-dressed diners eating at the Walnut Room, 1947. *ICHi-038786/Chicago History Museum/M.J. Schmidt, Photographer.*

Well-heeled customers arriving at the door would be greeted by a doorman. Inside, they could visit the store's beauty salon, children's playroom, travel service, post office station and theater ticket office. In the store's expansive waiting rooms, customers could meet friends, read national magazines and examine telephone directories from a hundred major American cities. Trained shoppers in the personal shopping service filled telephone and mail requests, averaging about ten thousand requests each day. The quiet elegance of the Walnut Room (originally named the South Grill Room) made it ideal for wealthy shoppers looking for a bite of chicken pot pie and a cup of tea, with perhaps a fashion show thrown in.

Kate Wells, who dyed her hair using a bottle of hydrogen peroxide and some ammonia when she heard the firm needed a blonde, worked as a Marshall Field's model for twelve years. "In the 1940s and '50s, Marshall Field and Company was noted for, among other things, its extravagant evening fashion shows held several times a year to benefit such Chicago organizations as the Opera Guild and the Art Institute," she said. "Marshall Field's also had more in-store fashion shows than any other department store in the United States."[31]

A Marshall Field's fashion show at the Ritz-Carlton benefiting the Rush-Presbyterian–St. Luke's Medical Center, September 1976. *ST-19110367-0024/*Chicago Sun-Times *Collection/Chicago History Museum.*

When Chicago's Municipal Airport (later renamed Midway) opened a new terminal in 1948, Marshall Field's established an elegant twenty-four-hour restaurant called the Cloud Room. It featured dramatic floor-to-ceiling views of the tarmac and delicacies such as pineapple flown in from Hawaii. For more than a decade, travelers arriving at Municipal Airport received their welcome to Chicago via the Cloud Room. Field's also ran the airport's informal Blue and Gold Café, said to be a favorite of Frank Sinatra. Midway's supremacy receded after O'Hare Airport opened in 1955, and the Cloud Room closed in 1962.

Its emphasis on luxury and indulgence helped Field's earn a rarified position as one of America's most prestigious, full-line department stores, alongside the Wanamaker department store in Philadelphia. The scale of Field's operations in the postwar era was spectacular. Marshall Field's trucks would deliver goods as far north as Waukegan, Illinois, and as far south as Gary, Indiana. During busy seasons, as many as nine thousand people worked at the downtown store.[32]

Much of the delight of shopping at Marshall Field's came from the experience itself. "Nylons came packaged in beautiful boxes with tissue paper wrapped around them. The saleslady would carefully open the box and slide in her hand to display how they would look on your skin. There were many choices of colors, shades, seams, no seams, reinforced toes or not…this was a very special shopping experience," remembered Carol Zetek Goddard.[33]

Not everyone, however, felt welcome. In Marshall Field's celebration year of 1952, a complaint was filed against it for discriminatory hiring practices. The firm's response to the Commission on Human Relations was that African American sales clerks would "negatively affect the character, atmosphere and flavor" of Marshall Field's. The company's argument that skin color was a legitimate hiring standard failed to convince the commission, which decided in favor of the complainant. Field's did hire African American staffers in the 1950s, but mostly for clerical, telephone sales and warehouse positions. At the end of the 1960s, only 9 percent of Marshall Field's salesforce was Black.[34]

Racial prejudice impacted customers too. Well into the twentieth century, African American shoppers experienced discrimination from sales clerks and other staffers at Field's. "We would be ignored or treated rudely and subjected to countless other racist indignities which are too numerous to go into here but which left you knowing that you were far from welcome as a Field's customer or as a human being," Joyce Miller Bean told a reporter in 2020.[35] Miller Bean remembered being ignored by clerks in the toy

James T. Palmer, president of Marshall Field's, stands in front of the company's new store at Old Orchard in Skokie, December 1958. *Francis Miller/The* LIFE *Picture Collection/Shutterstock.*

section and the anger and hatred shown by one sales clerk when her mother complained. For shoppers like her, visiting Marshall Field's at Christmas brought little of the same holiday joy it gave to others.

Marshall Field's had halted all expansion during the 1930s and '40s, but that changed at midcentury. Starting with the opening of the Park Forest Plaza branch in 1955, Field's began an aggressive push into suburban shopping malls. By 1962, the firm had branch stores in Skokie, Illinois; Oak Brook, Illinois; and Wauwatosa, Wisconsin.

Although the State Street Store continued to be the flagship, the company's attention increasingly was focused on its shopping-mall stores. Branch stores had more limited inventory, stocking primarily women's apparel and accessories, supplemented by men's and children's apparel, gifts and housewares. They lacked many of the amenities of the downtown store but were conveniently located, offered ample free parking and catered to the largely white, affluent customers flocking to the suburbs. Services like doormen and the children's playroom quietly disappeared from the downtown store.

The opening of Water Tower Place in 1975 gave Marshall Field's a presence in Chicago's posh Michigan Avenue shopping district. Four years later, a Marshall Field's store opened in Houston, Texas, marking the first time the Marshall Field's name appeared outside the Midwest.

Yet even as its expansion helped the Marshall Field's name remain dominant among Chicago department stores, the company's identity became increasingly difficult to distinguish. Merchandise became more standardized across other high-end department stores. Specialty stores began to outdraw Field's, especially among fashion-conscious customers. Competing department stores such as Lord and Taylor, I. Magnin and Neiman-Marcus moved into the Chicago area in the 1970s, cutting into Field's share of the upper-moderate to very upscale retail market.

Marshall Field's managed to remain independent through the 1970s, in part by acquiring other chains like Ohio-based Halle Brothers Company (acquired in 1970) and North Carolina–based J.B. Ivey and Company (1980) that made it less attractive to outside buyers. But by the early 1980s, the company was ripe for a hostile takeover. Marshall Field's executives began looking for a friendly buyer. They found it in BATUS (the U.S. division of BAT Industries, a U.K. tobacco firm). In 1982, BATUS acquired Marshall Field's and Frederick & Nelson for $310 million.[36]

The purchase marked the end of Marshall Field's as an independent, Chicago-based firm. BATUS quickly streamlined the company, selling off various chains, including Frederick & Nelson. The men's sections soon moved back into the main building. The Oak Park and Evanston branches closed in 1987.

But new ownership also brought new energy. Field's began carrying more upscale merchandise and a greater selection of unique items. The biggest renovation in Marshall Field's history began in 1987, when BATUS overhauled the State Street building in a five-year project costing more than $110 million. The renovation centered on a central, back-lit atrium with a dramatic escalator system. Major sections such as children's clothing moved to new locations. Shoppers spent months navigating drop cloths, but the renovations made the store dazzling again.

In 1990, BATUS sold Marshall Field's to the department store division of Dayton-Hudson Corporation (later renamed Target Corporation). Marshall Field's merchandise now shifted to more moderately priced products, to standardize with the Dayton's and Hudson's department stores. Many longtime customers bristled at the changes, especially the firm's heavy emphasis on promotions and the replacement of the store's signature dark green shopping bags with more environmentally friendly beige bags. In response, the company reinstated the green bags and cut back on promotions.

While visiting Chicago in September 1986, Charles, Prince of Wales, toured Marshall Field's and took part in a whiskey-blending demonstration using various Irish blends. *Mark Reinstein/Shutterstock.*

Disaster struck again in 1992. Workers repairing a bridge over the Chicago River accidentally punched into an ancient system of freight tunnels, sending water gushing through basements across downtown. When it reached Marshall Field's third subbasement, the electrical power failed, stalling the great clocks at 7:14 a.m.[37] Thanks to a massive effort to pump the water out, Field's State Street store reopened just five days later.

Marshall Field's gained a larger national profile in the early 2000s, when Dayton-Hudson changed the names of its Dayton's and Hudson's department stores to Marshall Field's. This brought the number of Marshall Field's stores nationwide to sixty-four stores in eight states. The company spruced up the downtown store, introduced more boutiques within the store and began a visual branding campaign using distinctive green stripes.

Overall, however, things looked gloomy. Like other department stores, Marshall Field's continued to struggle, buffeted by both strong competition and the weak economy at the time. Competition just kept mounting, from upscale retailers, from other department stores selling

Demonstrators protest in front of the former Marshall Field's department store on State Street, September 9, 2006. *REUTERS/Joshua Lott/Alamy Stock Photo.*

the same name-brand merchandise and from online merchants, who now emerged as a major threat. In 2004, the May Department Stores Company acquired Marshall Field's. One year later, May merged with Federated Department Stores.

The end came in September 2006, when Federated rebranded all Marshall Field's stores as Macy's. The Marshall Field's name disappeared, replaced by Macy's on storefronts, advertisements, shopping bags and gift boxes.

Many Chicagoans reacted with shock and anger. They began staging protests outside the State Street store, now known as Macy's on State Street. They picketed shareholders' meetings and called for boycotts. "You can go into other stores and buy stuff, but when you think about it, what is Chicago's best-known brand?" Jim McKay of Field's Fans Chicago (a grassroots group working to bring back Marshall Field's) asked DNAInfo.com. "There is a lot of nostalgia but also the idea of experiences coming back....Marshall Field's creates an experience that transcends shopping."[38]

Many things Chicagoans loved about Marshall Field's still remain. The iconic corner clocks are still there, as are the soaring light wells, the Tiffany mosaic and the bronze plaques bearing the store's original name. The grand building itself is both a National Historic Landmark and a Chicago City Landmark.

In a nod to Chicagoans' love of their hometown store, Macy's sells shirts, bags and other merchandise adorned with the Field's name, as well as green tins of Frango chocolates. "Frango mints are considered a Chicago institution," wrote Danny Miller in *Saveur* magazine. "Just give me an old-fashioned Frango mint and I am the picture of contentment."[39]

Marshall Field's left a remarkable legacy. More than any other Chicago department store, Marshall Field's showed that a department store could be more than just a place to spend money. It was a cherished public landmark, an awe-inspiring spectacle and a key part of Chicago's identity as one of the nation's greatest cities.

2.

CARSON PIRIE SCOTT

Carson's Is for Me

O f all the department stores in Chicago, the one that gave Marshall Field's a run for its money was Carson Pirie Scott and Company. Carson's, as it was familiarly dubbed, never matched Field's prestige. One writer jokingly dubbed it "the second store for the Second City,"[40] but it was very popular. Many shoppers carried credit cards for both stores, and the two companies shared a friendly but fierce competition.

They also shared nearly the same birthday. In 1854, just two years after Potter Palmer established his dry-goods business in Chicago, two young Scotsmen opened a store in tiny Amboy, Illinois, ninety miles west of Chicago.[41]

The two men were no strangers to relocating. Born in Glasgow, Scotland, John T. Pirie moved to Ireland at age fifteen to apprentice at his uncle's dry-goods store. While working there, he befriended another teenage apprentice named Samuel Carson.

The two young men, having decided to make their fortune together, sailed to the United States in 1854. After surviving a shipwreck off the coast of Newfoundland, they worked briefly at a store in New York before joining the westward migration. Their travels took them to Peru, Illinois, where they worked for brothers whose family they had known in Ireland.

By the next spring, they were in business for themselves, opening their store in nearby Amboy. The Amboy building, a small brick building with iron windows, sat on the town's main road, conveniently across from the railroad depot.

Store rules drawn up in the 1850s give a sense of the brothers' standards of conduct. Employees were required to participate in church and forbidden to habitually indulge in dancing, smoking Spanish cigars or being shaved at the barber's. Store hours were 6:00 a.m. to 9:00 p.m. year-round. Like other dry-goods businesses, Carson Pirie sold fabrics and fabric items. For women, they offered ginghams, French merino wools, calicos and light scarves called mantillas. For gentlemen, the store carried doeskins, pantaloons, woven wools, jeans and colored neckerchiefs.[42]

The partners prospered. Within four years, Carson and Pirie had branches in four nearby towns, making it one of the first American chain stores.[43] Two friends from Ireland, George and Robert Scott, became partners and added their name to the store in 1875. (Members of the founding families would remain involved for decades.)

At the end of the Civil War, the partners took the propitious step of opening a wholesale store in Chicago. Again, they prospered. Within three years, the first Carson Pirie Scott retail store in Chicago opened; in time, the company shuttered its other stores.

The company's shift to Chicago owed much to another Scottish immigrant. When Glasgow-born Andrew MacLeish arrived in Illinois, he ended up joining the company and spearheaded the move to Chicago in 1867.

MacLeish proved a hero in 1871 when the Great Chicago Fire swept through the city. According to one newspaper account, "Stationing himself at the side of the burning walls, he cupped his hands and shouted at passing teamsters. His offer of $50 cash per wagon load brought many volunteers and saved tons of merchandise from the hungry wind-swept flames."[44] Although an estimated 60 percent of the firm's goods burned, some $50,000 in merchandise was saved, and the company soon reopened.

From that time, Carson's grew steadily. The main Chicago retail store settled in 1883 at the southwest corner of Washington and State Streets, across from Marshall Field's. Then, in 1904, Carson Pirie Scott made its most significant move, relocating to a permanent home at State and Madison Streets.

Although Chicagoans still refer to the State and Madison store as "the Carson's building," it was not erected for Carson Pirie Scott but for a rival dry-goods business: Schlesinger & Mayer. Schlesinger & Mayer dated to 1872, just after the Great Chicago Fire, when German immigrants Leopold Schlesinger & David Mayer founded their namesake dry-goods firm. They prospered in Chicago's population boom of the 1880s and 1890s. By the 1890s, they had outgrown their existing building at State and Madison Streets.

An early Carson Pirie Scott building, 118–20 State Street, as seen in the late 1860s. Chicago Tribune *file photo*. Chicago Tribune *Archive Photos/TCA*.

The Carson Pirie Scott building at 1 South State Street (formerly Schlesinger & Mayer), photographed in July 1967. *Historic American Buildings Survey/Library of Congress.*

Schlesinger & Mayer approached the prominent architecture firm Adler and Sullivan to remodel and expand their existing store. When that proved impractical, they decided to start over. In 1899, they commissioned Louis Sullivan (whose partnership with Dankar Adler had ended in 1895) to design an entirely new building for them.

Sullivan enjoyed a reputation as the renegade who publicly rejected the classical, Beaux-Arts designs showcased at the 1893 World's Columbian Exposition. With his multihued, nonclassical Transportation Building at the exposition, Sullivan had declared himself the standout against rival Daniel H. Burnham, the exposition's chief of construction. Burnham would soon give Marshall Field's its grand, classically styled building.

Sullivan took an entirely different approach. He started with the site's particularly commanding position at the busy intersection of State and Madison. This is where the cable cars, and then later the electric trolley systems, crossed. It was the city's most iconic crossroads—and also its busiest. Sullivan's building showcased this intersection, as had the earlier building it replaced. The main entrance stood at the corner rather than the middle of the block, as was common in other stores. Its curving profile mirrored the curving of the streetcar tracks, which moved through the intersection of State and Madison in a similar swooping arc.[45] Sullivan then covered the rounded entrance with his signature ornamentation.

That ironwork, which extends along the building's lower level, gave shoppers a magically immersive experience. "Walking alongside the base of the building is akin to walking in a forest, the green of the flowing iron forms meant to evoke foliage dappled by sunlight," said architecture writer and tour guide Wendy Bright. Inside the store, you encounter "large 'trees' of mahogany in the vestibule, leading to rows of columns within the store, all topped with foliate capitals."[46]

Entrance to Carson Pirie Scott, circa 1907. View is looking east on Madison from State Street. Mandel Brothers is visible on the left. *Detroit Publishing Company/Library of Congress/ Prints and Photographs Division.*

With its steel-frame construction, the building qualified as a skyscraper, but it barely resembled other skyscrapers at the time. The profuse ironwork ornamentation covering the building's rounded entrance and its lower levels was complemented by the simplified, geometric lines of the upper floors, clad in smooth white terra-cotta. Extremely wide windows not only flooded the store's interiors with natural light but also gave the building its signature horizontal look.

Chicago architect John Randall explained, "[Sullivan] broke away from the usual traditional, stylistic treatment of the skyscraper and simplified and opened the façade....He expressed the structural framework and emphasized its heights, using frank and clean lines and planes."

Taken altogether, the building elegantly combines geometric and natural shapes. "No State Street department store, not even Marshall Field's, is more important in the history of architecture," wrote *Chicago Tribune* architecture critic Blair Kamin. "The Carson, Pirie, Scott and Company store was one of Louis Sullivan's greatest designs, perhaps his greatest, an epoch-defining image that transformed the static rationality of its structural steel frame into a superbly fluid composition that welcomes the shoppers with an intricate veil of cast iron ornament."[47]

The building went up in stages. The first part—a modest nine-story section with three window bays on Madison Street—opened in 1900. The much larger corner unit at State and Madison went up in 1903. Schlesinger & Mayer trumpeted the opening of their new building in gloriously illustrated full-page newspaper ads. The fanfare, however, hid the fact that, by this point, the firm was struggling under a mountain of financial pressures. In 1904, they decided to call it quits.

Harry G. Selfridge, the energetic head of Marshall Field's retail operations, stepped in. Itching to run his own company, Selfridge left Field's to go into business for himself. Schlesinger & Mayer sold him their building and merchandise for a princely $5 million. Newspaper ads in June 1904 trumpeted the "birth of a new business" named H.G. Selfridge and Company.

Two months later, Selfridge was gone. He had sold his business to Carson Pirie Scott.

What happened? Selfridge explained it with a shrug. "There is not much to say. Carson, Pirie, Scott and Co. offered me a large bonus over and above what I paid for the business about eight weeks ago and I have taken it."[48] Insiders speculated that Selfridge found it uncomfortable competing with his longtime friends nearby at Field's. Selfridge would reemerge in 1909, when he opened Selfridge's department store in London.

Schlesinger & Mayer grand opening advertisement, *Chicago Tribune*, October 12, 1903.

Selfridge's loss was Carson's gain. With the move to the Sullivan building in 1904, Carson Pirie Scott gained not only a top-notch location but also a building that was architecturally even more impressive than Marshall Field's. Like its rivals, Carson's pampered its customers. Shoppers could enjoy amenities like the third-floor restroom filled with comfortable rocking chairs and abundant green plants. A pedestrian bridge let customers enter directly from the elevated trains into the store. Like Field's, Carson's ran buses back and forth from the various train stations.

Unlike Field's, however, Carson Pirie Scott mostly targeted the middle class. "Field's tended to appeal to the higher-end shopper, or at least those who harbored such aspirations, while Carson's reached out to the middle class," explained historian Gayle Soucek.[49] The middle class was the fastest-growing segment of Chicago's ever-expanding population in this era. Early advertisements touted Carson's not as a luxurious cathedral of consumption but as the "Store of Compactness, Convenience, Comfort and Good Merchandise."[50]

That is not to say Carson's did not carry merchandise for high-end shoppers. One 1925 advertisement featured women's coats with embroidered collars and cuffs in red or tan for $125.00 ($1,654.00 in 2021 dollars). Still, most Carson's merchandise fell into the moderate to slightly higher range. That same 1925 advertisement also included boys' suits for $2.25 (about $34.00 today).[51]

Carson's middle-of-the-market approach proved shrewd. Over the years, the store's growing customer base required it to keep expanding physically. In 1906, officials hired Burnham to design an addition with five more window bays extending down State Street. Additional buildings eventually extended the store all the way to Wabash Avenue on the east.

Many of Carson's innovations were driven by its ongoing competition with Marshall Field's. When Field's broke ground in 1949 for a branch in pioneering Park Forest Plaza, Carson's soon announced it too would be opening a shopping center branch store, in Evergreen Park's Evergreen Plaza. That store, Carson's first venture into the suburbs, opened in 1952.

When Marshall Field's announced it had purchased 110 acres of land in Skokie to be developed into a shopping mall, Caron's officials quickly announced plans to develop their own shopping center, to be called Edens Plaza. Located in North Shore Wilmette, it included a 130,000-square-foot Carson Pirie Scott store. At almost the same time, store officials announced plans for Carson's to be the largest tenant in another new shopping center in Hillside, to complement the newly opened Congress (later Eisenhower) Expressway.

Over the next few decades, as shopping centers opened across the metropolitan area, most of them would have either a Marshall Field's or a Carson Pirie Scott anchor store, but only in a few instances both.

Carson's College Almanac

Fundamentals for Fall: exciting, inviting skirts for collegiennes, careerists ... to live in and love

. . . By Madison Sportswear, natur-ally! Wonderful wardrobe back-bones ...enduring, endearing for versatility, verve and fine fabric. Misses' sizes.

(A) Fransworth's Tweed Tunnel Looper. Taupe, gold or grey, leather belt-ed, 10-18. **12.95**

(B) Fly front-back basic. Brown, red, gold, purple green, white. 10-18. **12.95** Matching Stole. **7.95**

(C) Dovella belted flannel. Black, navy, grey, dark green or brown. 10-20. **10.95**

(D) Kick-pleated flannel, smartly belted, Oxford brown, light or dark grey, 10-18. **12.95**

(E) Trouser tucked checks. Sheer wool, brown or purple combinations,10-18. **9.95**

(F) Authentic Tartan. Slim, trim in Munroe Ancient (red), MacHardy (navy), 10-18. **12.95**

College Almanac Fashions, Fourth Floor

Mail orders invited . . . Carson Pirie Scott & Co., Chicago, d 15c postage per item outside delivery area.

Left: Like other department stores, Carson's advertised in national magazines, inviting mail orders from shoppers outside the Chicago area. *Mademoiselle*, August 1951.

Below: Cars pack the parking lot for opening day of the Carson Pirie Scott store at Edens Plaza, Wilmette, May 1956. *Wilmette Historical Museum.*

C. Virgil Martin, president of Carson's in 1961, confidently predicted that suburban shopping center stores would lure new customers to State Street. "In 1954, before we opened [a branch in Hammond, Indiana], we had exactly 700 charge accounts in Lake County, Indiana," Martin explained. "Today we have about 27,000 to 28,000 charge accounts there and we're getting a tremendous amount of business downtown from these new customers."[52]

Martin's optimism proved premature. The rapid growth of outlying shopping centers, combined with ongoing congestion and inadequate parking in the downtown area, were double-barreled problems for downtown stores. Despite vigorous efforts by the State Street Council to promote downtown shopping, by the mid-1950s, Carson's officials seriously contemplated abandoning the State Street store altogether.

Their decision to stay—and more than that, to purchase the building that they had been leasing for more than fifty years—reassured many Chicagoans that the region's retailing would remain centered on State Street.[53] Nonetheless, the majority of Carson's growing profits continued to come from the shopping center stores. By the 1960s, Carson's had eleven stores around the Chicago region.

Carson's scored a coup in 1963, when it nabbed a deal to run the restaurants in the rotunda building at newly completed O'Hare Airport. Carson's hoped a restaurant at the airport would do for them what the restaurants at Chicago's Municipal Airport had done for Marshall Field's. Built at a cost of nearly $6 million, the rotunda building boasted four dining rooms, the most luxurious of which was the Seven Continents Restaurant, where diners could feast on live lobster, Russian caviar and escargots, much of it flown in daily by jet. Circular glass walls provided a sweeping view of the airfield. Carson's operated not only the Seven Continents but also the three other dining spaces at O'Hare, capable of seating 1,200 persons at a time.[54]

The Seven Continents was just one of Carson's ongoing efforts to stay up to date, in both its merchandise and its look. In 1948, the State Street store's floating cornice was removed, giving the building a more midcentury, streamlined feel. When the State Street store's two eighth-floor restaurants—a tearoom and a separate men's grill—were deemed outdated in 1959, they were replaced with an elegant new restaurant called the Heather House. The new restaurant's centerpiece was a fifty-foot, hand-painted panoramic mural depicting the city of Edinburgh, Scotland, as it looked around 1880.

Pedestrians enjoy hot dogs during a National Kraut and Frankfurter Week promotion on Chicago's State Street in January 1964. *Kim Vintage Stock/Alamy.*

The Heather House catered to female tastes, with an emphasis on light luncheons and afternoon tea, often accompanied by fashion shows. Among the Heather House's most popular offerings were chicken pot pie, shrimp salad served in a pineapple shell, homemade cinnamon buns and the Heather House pie, consisting of vanilla ice cream in a graham cracker shell, topped by toasted meringue and served with hot butter rum sauce. A generous slice cost sixty cents in 1969.[55]

Postcard view of the Heather House restaurant inside Carson Pirie Scott's State Street store, opened 1959.

Along with the Heather House, many other beloved Carson's traditions solidified in the midcentury era. Shopping for Christmas presents and visiting Santa Claus at Carson Pirie Scott became an annual tradition for many Chicagoans. The auditorium provided space year-round for fashion shows, celebrity appearances and other special store events. Hallways leading to the auditorium featured publicity photographs of celebrities who had visited the store over the years. Autograph signings by celebrities took place not in the auditorium but at the store's French writing desk on the third floor, just inside the spectacular rotunda window.

The 1960s saw the opening of some Carson's stores on Sundays, a development that would have been unthinkable in the early 1900s. But officials yielded to public pressure. "We wish we didn't have to do it," a spokesman regretfully told the *Chicago Tribune*. "But families are making an all-day outing of shopping. This is the only day they can all get together."[56] By the 1970s, all the big department stores had regular Sunday hours.

Carson Pirie Scott suffered badly on March 29, 1968, when suspicious fires broke out at several department stores on State Street, including the Carson's store. Some twenty-five thousand spectators converged on State and Madison Streets during the lunch hour that day as rumors spread that State Street was burning. The most serious fire had erupted on Carson's sixth floor, where art and picture frames were sold. The fire-suppression system on that floor had been disabled for ongoing remodeling work, and the blaze leapt quickly to the seventh floor. Firefighters shattered large windows on the sixth floor to pour water onto the flames. Other fires broke out at the Wieboldt's and Montgomery Ward stores on State Street but caused only minor damage. The Carson's fire was the worst, causing millions of dollars in damage.

Carson Pirie Scott never lost sight of its target customer. Glenn I. Larson, who became general manager of the State Street store in 1976, said, "We try to appeal to a relatively broad customer base, neither low-income nor exceptionally high-income, but moderate-to-upper income," he explained. "We would cross over both Field's and Goldblatt's boundaries."

That moderate-to-upper-income base increasingly included Chicago's ethnic and racial minority groups, whose numbers were growing. In 1976, the best-performing Carson's suburban branch was the Evergreen Plaza store, which Larson had managed. "One important characteristic of the Evergreen Plaza store may stand Larson in good stead downtown," predicted the *Chicago Tribune*. "The suburban facility attracted a high percentage of black shoppers, and black shoppers in the Loop are a growing proportion of the big department stores' customers."[57]

Left: Carson Pirie Scott enjoyed a strong reputation for fashion. This dress, designed by Anne Fogarty, retailed for $29.95 in 1957 (about $290.00 today).

Below: Postcard view of the main aisle at Carson Pirie Scott's State Street store, decorated for Christmas, circa 1960.

Josephine Baskin Minow remembered working with Focus, a group formed by Chicago race-relations pioneer Eleanor Peterson in the 1970s. "One of our goals was to integrate the staffs of those downtown department stores where hardly anyone of color was to be seen in the sales staff, in ads, the fashion shows, or as the window and floor models," she said. "Carson Pirie Scott was ahead of the pack but the others were very slow to come around."

By the 1980s, Carson's had earned a devoted following. The spectacular State Street building's architecture and its distinctive Sullivanesque foliage continued to draw admiration, and its middle-class focus continued to draw a devoted following, which the company capitalized on in its 1980s slogan, "Carson's Is for Me!" At one point, Carson's had eight thousand employees and did approximately $150 million in annual sales.[58]

"My mother's favorite store to shop at was Carson's," explained blogger Les Raff, who remembered taking the elevated train into the city to shop with her.

The day would always wind up at Carson's. When Mom was done with her purchases there, laden with shopping bags, we would head to the basement and the Tartan Tray Cafeteria....Sliding our trays along, we would pick out a sweet treat, a glass beaker of coffee for Mom and some tea for me, before searching out a table in the crowded seating area. Since then, I have had many meals in [modern] department store restaurants...but they don't hold a candle to those almost forgotten department store restaurant memories.[59]

Carson's always strove to remain modern and up-to-date while honoring its historic roots. In 1979, as part of the company's 125th anniversary celebration, the entrance rotunda was restored. Workers stripped away decades of paint and modern wood paneling and repainted the entire space, allowing modern shoppers to experience the delicate, lacelike iron- and plasterwork in their original colors.[60] The building was designated a Chicago City Landmark in 1970 and a National Historic Landmark in 1975.

A push to acquire more fashionable merchandise in the early 1980s paid off. A posh new Corporate Level, opened in 1985, lured executives to shop in a mirrored space with extended hours. "In the 80s, their State Street men's department was incredible. Top-notch style and quality," recalled shopper Greg Jones.[61]

Carson's also purchased an airline catering and restaurant chain and acquired a national chain of 276 clothing stores for teenagers called the County Seat. By the mid-1980s, Carson's owned 21 other department stores, mostly in northern Illinois.

But pressure continued to mount. After fending off an investment group and merging with Donaldson's department stores in Minneapolis, Carson's was finally acquired in 1989 by P.A. Bergner and Company, a regional chain of midwestern stores. The large debt that Bergner's took on to acquire Carson's eventually helped push it into bankruptcy. Carson's subsequently underwent a number of ownership changes before being purchased by the Bon-Ton chain of department stores in 2006.

Many Chicagoans were heartbroken when Bon-Ton decided, soon after acquiring Carson's, that the famous State Street store would close in March 2007. Although the remaining Carson's stores remained open, even the 260-store Bon-Ton empire could not buck the tide. In April 2018, Bon-Ton declared bankruptcy, sold its assets and announced the closing of its remaining stores.[62]

Chicagoans reacted with grief and shock. "I just can't believe this could happen," said longtime shopper Karen Wassilak of Algonquin, Illinois. "I hate to see it go."[63]

Customers shop on the main floor of the Carson Pirie Scott store after the retailer was sold to Bon-Ton, March 2006. *Phil Velasquez*/Chicago Tribune. Chicago Tribune *Archive Photos*/TCA.

"It's a real shame," agreed McHenry, Illinois resident Catherine Erwin. "A lot of people I knew when they were first starting their careers would need to go get at least one really good suit. Where did you go? You went to Field's; you went to Carson's. Those are the places you went to find those nicer pieces."[64]

Carson's fan Marina Tabor summed it up well. "Walking into Carson was like visiting family—pleasant, familiar, and always a warm welcome like you belong. There will never be a place like it anymore."[65]

3.

THE FAIR

Everything for Everybody Under One Roof

*She realized in a dim way how much the city held—wealth, fashion, ease—every
adornment for women, and she longed for dress and beauty with a whole heart.*
—*Theodore Dreiser,* Sister Carrie

Theodore Dreiser's 1900 novel *Sister Carrie* opens with the young Caroline
Meeber traveling to Chicago from her small country hometown.
Before long, needing a job, she seeks work in a Chicago department
store, and a policeman directs her to The Fair. She enters the massive store
and wanders up and down the aisles, awestruck by the displays of enticing
trinkets, dress goods, stationery and jewelry. "There was nothing there
which she could not have used—nothing which she did not long to own."[66]

Marshall Field's was grander. Sears was bigger. But many historians
consider The Fair Chicago's first true department store: a large-scale store
with multiple departments that sold "everything for everybody."

In 1873, German-born Ernst Lehmann launched The Fair when he took
over a modest one-story frame building on the west side of State Street.
Using his modest $1,000 capital, he filled the 1,280-square-foot store with
affordable jewelry, notions, chinaware, hardware and kitchen utensils. Over
the entrance, he hung a sign as economical as his store itself. It simply read,
"The Fair / Cheap."

Unlike elite department stores that grew from traditional dry-goods
stores, The Fair began as a multidepartment retailer selling many different
kinds of merchandise under one roof. Like the other discount department
stores that would follow it, The Fair served working-class Chicagoans,

better-off immigrants and budget-minded members of the middle class. Its merchandise and advertising emphasized low prices and large inventory, not luxury.

The Fair opened during a national economic depression, and its no-frills approach suited the time. Lehmann named his store "The Fair" for two reasons. First, he said, it conveyed that the store would deal fairly with its customers. Second, it would be like a fair in offering an endlessly varied assortment of merchandise.

This approach relied on high volume—many sales at small profits—and prices that undercut other stores. Most merchants who bought an item for, say, five cents, would sell it for ten cents, but Lehmann was willing to use "odd prices," selling that same item for a thrifty six or seven cents. He also advertised enthusiastically, plastering his buildings with promotional signs and placing the first full-page advertisement for a department store in a Chicago newspaper.

According to the store's 1915 promotional book *Since Forty Years Ago*, this approach revolutionized "the whole history of Retailing." The book summed up The Fair's entire approach in one sentence: "Everything for Everybody under one roof, at a lower price—and that price an odd price."[67]

That bargain-proclaiming odd price—combined with a staggeringly wide variety of goods—proved enormously appealing. By 1877, Lehmann had absorbed the next store to the north on State Street. Then, in 1878, he took over the store to the south. Soon after that, he snapped up two vacant stores on Adams, and then several more.

Like other discount department stores of the late nineteenth century, The Fair sold for cash only, which helped drive its success. Credit was common at the time in small-town general stores, where merchants kept running accounts that customers settled on a monthly or annual basis. A cash-only retailer fit better in a big city, where it was difficult to measure a customer's financial ability.[68] Like other cash stores, including The Boston Store in Chicago, Macy's in New York and Bon Marché in Seattle, Lehmann could sell for lower prices because he did not offer credit and did not have the additional expenses associated with credit customers.

To maintain the flow, Lehmann purchased in big quantities, often buying out the stock of closing stores and adding the merchandise to his store as a new department. The Fair's steady physical growth reflected its need for space to hold this abundance of merchandise as it absorbed one building after another.

E. J. LEHMANN'S TRIUMPH

Is a Triumph for His Customers,

And Shows That the People Appreciate the Fact Where the Best Goods for the Least Money Can Always Be Had.

BARGAINS DIRECT FROM ALL PARTS OF THE WORLD.

The Public Approval, the Result of Ten Years' Trade.

Advertisement for The Fair, *Chicago Tribune*, May 31, 1885.

In 1886, the business had grown sufficiently complex that Lehmann decided to incorporate, a move that increased his funding and allowed him to begin an aggressive rebuilding scheme. The hodge-podge collection of buildings would be replaced by a single grand structure. In 1890, he announced that the wrecking ball would swing that summer in anticipation of a jaw-droppingly huge, nine-story, $2 million building.

When completed in 1897, the steel-and-terra-cotta building boasted 677,550 square feet of space, 31,700 feet of counters and two immense light shafts that flooded the building with daylight. The corner window at State and Adams Streets was trumpeted as the largest show window in the country. A team of three thousand employees was needed to staff what was, briefly, "the largest and grandest store in the world," at least until Macy's in New York overtook it in 1902.[69]

The new building had fewer frills than Marshall Field's or Schlesinger & Mayer's forthcoming buildings would, but The Fair was no longer strictly no-frills. Competition among stores on State Street by this era, as well as the continuing rise in the standard of living among many Chicagoans, compelled store executives to add more amenities and more high-end items. While still billing itself as the "store of the people," The Fair expanded its offerings. By 1891, The Fair sold toys, baby carriages, furniture, sewing machines and kitchen equipment. By 1914, shoppers could take advantage of the in-store post office branch, writing room, dental parlor, spacious waiting room, nursery, free wrapping counters and free checkroom.[70] To better appeal to Chicago's middle-class shoppers, The Fair now offered credit, leaving behind the strictly cash policy of early years so it could expand its customer base.

High volume still remained key to The Fair's success. In the early 1900s, a team of buyers scoured the United States, as well as England, Scotland, Ireland, France, Austria, Switzerland, Germany and other foreign markets for goods. *Since Forty Years Ago* tells how The Fair once purchased twenty carloads' worth of writing tablets, "probably the largest single purchase of stationery ever made by a retail store." Another time, it brought in 4,950 trunks. "When the bicycle was the real speed king, The Fair sold as many as one thousand of them in a single day."[71] By the 1910s, The Fair had 800,000 square feet of floor space and employed 5,500 workers, making it one of the city's largest employers.

Lehmann himself, however, suffered health problems, said to be caused by overwork and mental stress. His wife gained authority to have him committed to a mental institution in 1890, where he passed away in 1900.[72] Family members continued to run The Fair until 1925, when they sold it to

Entrances to The Fair's State Street store, 1945. *HB-08744-A/Chicago History Museum/ Hedrich-Blessing Collection.*

The Fair branch store at Randhurst Center in Mount Prospect, circa 1962. *Mount Prospect Historical Society.*

a syndicate headed by dime-store magnate S.S. Kresge, creator of one of the twentieth century's largest discount chain stores, S.S. Kresge and Company.

Kresge kept a largely hands-off approach, and The Fair continued to flourish in the booming 1920s economy. In 1929, The Fair was one of the first Chicago department stores to open branch locations, first on Milwaukee Avenue and then in suburban Oak Park. In the 1950s, the firm added additional locations in Evergreen Park and Skokie.

By the 1950s, however, retail shopping had changed dramatically. The retail environment favored large department store chains with a regional or even national profile. That made smaller local chains like The Fair ripe for takeover by national chains.

It came in 1957. Retail giant Montgomery Ward, with an eye toward expanding its Chicago-based operations, purchased The Fair. Ward initially kept the name The Fair, even adding one more branch store, in 1962 at Randhurst shopping center in suburban Mount Prospect. But the writing was on the wall. The Randhurst store operated for less than a year under The Fair name before converting to the Montgomery Ward name in August 1963. By 1964, all the other locations had converted to the Ward name. The flagship building stood until 1984, when it was demolished. With that, little remained of The Fair other than memories of what many consider the city's first true department store.

4.

MONTGOMERY WARD

Satisfaction Guaranteed or Your Money Back

When Aaron Montgomery Ward launched his mail-order company in 1872, the United States' population totaled only about forty-two million people, the vast majority of them living in rural areas. The 1870 census showed that three-quarters of Americans lived on farms or in towns of fewer than 2,500 people.[73]

These residents of rural areas often found themselves living isolated lives. How isolated you were varied a bit, depending on weather and topography, but many states had a population density that averaged fewer than twenty-five people per square mile. No radio, television or other mass communication connected homesteaders with the larger world.

The same era that saw settlers and homesteaders moving westward to improve the land—roughly 1865 to 1915—also saw American manufacturers enjoying their own era of expansive growth and transformation. In the years just before and after the American Civil War, newly invented products were being manufactured in quantities never before imagined. The same manufacturing methods pioneered by Eli Whitney and Samuel Colt to make guns and revolvers now churned out clocks, cultivators, sewing machines and countless other things faster, better and cheaper than ever before.

The ideal customers for these new products? Those settlers and homesteaders living far from big stores. And the first person to tap into the buying potential of this vast retail market was a young man from New Jersey named Aaron Montgomery Ward.

Ward was still in his twenties when he ventured west to begin working for several big-city wholesalers, including the leading Chicago dry-goods house Field, Palmer and Leiter, which offered its customers a pioneering money-back guarantee. He also worked for a St. Louis wholesaler that sent him out to drum up sales from country stores.

As he traveled across the Midwest, selling goods to owners of general stores, Ward chatted with storekeepers and their customers. He heard farmers complain about the limited selection of goods and high prices in small-town stores.

Ward was inspired. What if he opened a mail-order company to serve rural customers? His home base could be in a big city, where it was easier to receive and ship out a large stock of goods. Customers could pick out what they wanted from a list of available goods, and Ward would mail the merchandise to them. He wouldn't need salesmen. He wouldn't need a fancy store.

He could sell to anyone in America. And with that big a customer base, he could buy goods from manufacturers in enormous quantities—meaning he'd get a lower price. Customers would get a much wider selection of goods at significantly lower prices.

There had been mail-order catalogs before, typically for businesses selling one type of merchandise by mail. Benjamin Franklin reportedly created the first mail-order catalog in the United States, a listing of six hundred valuable books. Tiffany issued its first catalog, featuring exceedingly rare gems, in 1845. But no one had ever offered a full line of goods—and sold them exclusively by mail.

Ward had supreme confidence in his vision. He later wrote, "Having had experience in all classes of merchandise [as a] traveling salesman, and [being] a fair judge of human nature, I saw a great opening for a house to sell direct to the consumer and save them the profit of the middle man."[74]

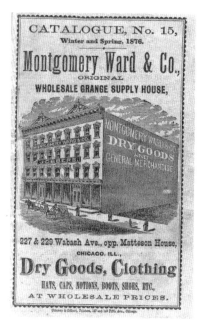

The cover of the fifteenth Montgomery Ward catalog, winter/spring 1876, shows the building that was then its Chicago headquarters. Note the phrase "Original Wholesale Grange Supply House."

To give his new business credibility, Ward teamed up with a newly created fraternal organization, the Patrons of Husbandry. Better known as the Grange, it worked to support and promote America's agricultural communities. At about the time Ward launched his business, there were more than twenty thousand Granges with about eight hundred thousand members. Ward convinced their leaders to make him the official Grange supply house, giving him a patina of credibility—and access to an enormous mailing list.

Ward was set to mail out his first price list in October 1871, when the Great Chicago Fire burned much of downtown Chicago, including Ward's small supply of merchandise. Undeterred, he scraped together funds to start over.

The next year, in August 1872, Ward and his brother-in-law George Thorne put together the first Montgomery Ward and Company catalog: a single sheet crammed with 163 items and their prices. There were no pictures and only brief descriptions of each item.

It worked. Farm families sent in orders, and soon others did, too. The catalog slowly caught on. To reach farmers, Ward ran ads in farm newspapers and packed his catalog with windmills, corn planters, farm wagons, plows, harnesses and motors of all kinds. Sewing machines were the catalog's bestseller. Ward's enormous buying power let him keep prices ridiculously low, sometimes half of what retail stores charged.

As Ward's customer base grew, so did the catalog, and with it the space for describing the goods. Ward proved to be a natural here as well, combining plain talk and old-time aphorisms with friendly salesmanship. Everything about the catalog stressed the company's honesty and commitment to good value. To explain the low prices, Ward stated, "We don't pay $40,000 a year rent. We don't employ high-priced salesmen. Our goods are bought direct from manufacturers."[75] And everything came with an ironclad guarantee: "Satisfaction guaranteed or your money back!" The company would even pay post on returned merchandise. Catalogs showed pictures of Ward himself and his key managers to reassure customers they were dealing with real people.

It was, historian Russell Lewis, explained, a truly revolutionary idea. Ward proved "that you can sell products to customers you never saw, and people would buy things they never touched or held."[76] And it all meshed perfectly with the era—the innovative use of railroad delivery, wholesome salesmanship and the innovative way prices stayed low. It is small wonder that *Forbes* included Aaron Montgomery Ward on its 2005 list of the twenty most influential businessmen of all time.[77]

Montgomery Ward's catalog for 1904–5 celebrated rural free delivery of U.S. mail. *Chicago History Museum/Alamy Stock.*

And Ward wasn't done. As printing technology developed, so did the catalog. Item descriptions grew more detailed. He added illustrations. In 1874, the catalog had 32 pages. By 1876, it had 152 pages; by 1899, a whopping 1,076 pages. By then, the catalog was going out to 729,000 homes.

Country shopkeepers fought back, railing against mail order. Some even staged public burnings of mail-order catalogs, but Ward always emphasized the company's honesty: "If any of your goods are not satisfactory after due inspection, we will take them back, pay all expenses and refund the money paid for them."[78]

Mail-order shopping transformed life in America's farm communities, and as the catalog grew, so did its importance in American farmers' lives. Country schoolhouse teachers used the catalog in their lessons, teaching math by having students fill out order forms and geography by using the catalog's postal maps. Girls cut up old catalogs to make paper dolls. New catalogs brought information about new farm machines, new fashions and new time-saving gadgets.

Changing postal technologies proved critical in helping Ward's mail-order business grow. Rural free delivery of mail began in 1896, allowing even farm families to have their newspapers, letters and catalogs delivered right to their homes. In 1912, parcel post delivery began. Prior to that, shoppers had to pick up their orders at the postal office or the railroad station or use private companies for any parcel weighing more than four pounds. Now, customers could have packages, even those weighing more than four pounds, delivered to their door. On the day parcel post service began, Ward's wagons rushed to the post office with forty bags of parcels to be the first Chicago business to use the new service.

Monkey Ward's, as many customers jokingly called the company, brought a cornucopia of dreams to people living in remote corners of a young country. During the heyday of mail order in the 1890s and early 1900s, Montgomery Ward churned out thick catalogs packed with enticing merchandise that would be shipped out quickly. One longtime Ward customer remembered, "When I was a child, the arrival of Ward catalogs was like having Christmas come three or four times a year."[79]

The 1895 Ward's catalog, at 624 pages, carried tens of thousands of items: a toy wagon for $1.70, a doll carriage for $0.45, seven styles of trunks ranging from $0.50 to $4.00, a deluxe sewing machine for $20.80, mechanical toys, sofas, high-button shoes, flat irons, ice-cream freezers, bathtubs and fine china. The company barely exaggerated when it said its catalog offered "most every article required by the civilized world."[80]

The company opened several mail-order branches to help merchandise get to customers more quickly. In Chicago, it built a twelve-story building at 6 North Michigan Avenue to serve as the flagship fulfillment center and headquarters. Topped with a gilded weathervane statue of a torch-wielding woman titled *Progress Lighting the Way for Commerce*, the structure opened in 1899 as the tallest commercial building in the world.

Farm families visiting Chicago for the World's Columbian Exposition found the Montgomery Ward building as enticing as the fair itself. City folks might want to see Marshall Field's, but rural folk descended on the Montgomery Ward headquarters. Ward's had become an American tradition.

But it had also been bypassed by its young competitor, Sears, Roebuck. Backed by Richard Sears's tireless advertising and enthusiastic trumpeting of low prices, Sears overtook Ward's in annual sales in 1900 and never looked back. Between 1902 and 1906, Sears' mail-order business grew at double the rate of Ward's.[81]

Still, Montgomery Ward continued to grow. With congestion on Michigan Avenue growing, Ward executives bought property along the Chicago River near the Chicago Avenue bridge and built an expansive new catalog plant. The building, Chicago's first large, reinforced concrete structure, took more than two years to erect and spanned five hundred feet along the riverbank when completed in 1908.[82] Inside, miles of chutes and conveyor belts shuttled goods around. Covered railroad tracks could accommodate two trains of sixty-six cars each simultaneously.

Montgomery Ward had by this time withdrawn from active participation in the business. He sold his controlling interest in the company to Thorne, as his attention was increasingly focused on preserving Chicago's lakefront opposite the downtown area as a city park. When he died in December 1913, the *Chicago Tribune* declared Ward "the watchdog of the lakefront."[83]

The company branched out in the 1910s, introducing automobile parts and even, briefly, an automobile itself, the Modoc. It began to do more manufacturing, especially of farm equipment such as cream separators and gasoline engines.

The company kept its focus on its target customers: rural farmers and small-town Americans. By this point, the firm could boast an impressively loyal customer base. One lonesome rancher even wrote to inquire about a drawing of a model he had seen in the catalog. He wanted a wife, so would Ward's please send him number 1242?[84]

During World War I, the company faced some challenges, especially as government regulations and shortages of goods, not to mention unreliable shipping, created headaches for mail-order firms. The company abandoned its cash-only policy and began selling certain items on installment.

After the war, inflation and falling commodity prices gave the firm even more challenges. The company ended 1920 with a loss, the first in its history. Groceries, once a big seller, disappeared in 1926. Ready-cut homes sold under the name Wardway were dropped in 1931, a casualty of the economy.

The biggest challenge, however, was waning mail order. Farm populations were shrinking, while improved roads and affordable automobiles were causing small towns to blossom. Some wondered if mail order had gone as far as it could.

Vice-President Robert E. Wood thought so. After pouring over census figures and studying demographic charts, he proposed that Ward's begin opening retail stores to build on its well-known name, huge buying power

A typical Montgomery Ward store in Urbana, Illinois, 1949. *Champaign County Historical Archives/The Urbana Free Library.*

and large distribution centers. The company demurred, and Wood left for Sears. Under Wood's direction, Sears moved ahead aggressively into the retail store field starting in the mid-1920s.

Montgomery Ward executives finally—and reluctantly—agreed to experiment. In 1926, they opened modest "display" stores in three small towns: one in Indiana, one in Kansas and one in Minnesota. The stores displayed merchandise customers could examine and compare, but all orders would be shipped. That plan crumbled when customers complained about not being able to take goods home. Combative customers who refused to take no for an answer finally pushed Ward's into selling directly to in-store customers.

Although Ward executives grumbled that the stores would take business from mail order, the company now embarked on an ambitious retail store expansion plan. The firm clung to its target rural customer base, opening stores in small towns and mid-sized cities and shying away from the large metropolitan regions.

Wood had been right. The retail stores had muscle. In 1928, catalog sales sputtered, but retail sales already topped $60 million. By the end of 1929, the company had 531 retail stores across the country. Still, as retail consultant Sid Doolittle later explained: "It was a reaction, not a positive strategic change for Ward's. And they were reacting all the way from there on."[85]

The Great Depression hit mail order hard, and sales continued to tumble during the 1930s. Retail-store sales dropped, too, although less dramatically, and retail permanently overtook mail order in 1930. By the time businessman Sewell Avery stepped in as chairman of the board, chief executive officer and general manager in 1931, more than 450 of the 610 Ward stores were losing money, and the original catalog business continued to slide.

Avery moved decisively. He reorganized the company, reclassifying merchandise by quality categories, centralizing control and speeding up some store expansion. He brought in sharp-minded young retail minds to hone the company's merchandising, operations and retail sales. *Fortune* magazine in January 1935 declared the turnaround "a notable rejuvenation of the Ward company."[86]

Avery steered Montgomery Ward through the Great Depression in decent shape. By 1939, when the company had 618 stores, sales were moving consistently upward again. Telephone ordering was now established, and Ward's catalogs also shone, with more color pages than ever.

Ward's sales held steady during the war, despite shortages, government-regulated price ceilings and Avery's bitter distrust of Franklin D. Roosevelt's policies. In April 1944, when Avery refused to comply with wartime labor agreements, Roosevelt ordered a government takeover of the Chicago plant, to be run for the government. In the face of Avery's resistance, the government sent soldiers, who literally carried him out of the Montgomery Ward administration building. Newspapers across the country carried front-page photographs of the event the next day.

An even bigger challenge, however, emerged after the war. Convinced that growing demands for consumer goods would not last and that a recession was just over the horizon, Avery hunkered down.[87] He halted all plans for new stores and shut down funding for modernizations, hoping that squirreling away cash would help Ward's survive an impending financial blow. He refused to install air-conditioning or even paint the increasingly shabby, older stores.

Sears took exactly the opposite path, opening new stores on a massive scale and riding the tide of America's postwar economic boom to enormous profits. As suburbs blossomed across the nation, Sears stores seemed to pop up in every one, ready to serve them.

Soldiers carry Sewell Avery, chairman of Montgomery Ward, out of his office on October 31, 1944, after he refused to cooperate with government officials who took over the firm during World War II. *Harry Hall/AP/Shutterstock.*

Into the 1950s, most Montgomery Ward stores were still small stores in small towns. Almost two-thirds of them were in towns with fewer than twenty-five thousand residents. They, and the Montgomery Ward brand itself, looked increasingly dowdy. The majority of Montgomery Ward stores lacked modern amenities now considered standard.

Avery's autocratic reign ended with his resignation in 1955, leaving the firm, as *Fortune* magazine put it, "the shell of a once great company."[88] Led first by chairman John A. Barr and then, after Barr's retirement in 1965, by Robert E. Brooker, new management in the late 1950s rolled up its sleeves and got to work. They launched a feverish effort to modernize Ward's retail stores, closing unprofitable sites and expanding into suburban shopping malls, although Sears and J.C. Penney had already snapped up prime locations. Once again, Ward's had to play catch-up.

Nonetheless, Ward's seemed to be on the move again. Fifty new stores opened between 1958 and 1961, and hundreds of smaller existing stores got facelifts. Ward's expansive mall stores often featured automobile service centers, garden shops, coffee shops, candy counters and banks of catalogs for telephone ordering.

Montgomery Ward executives focused most of their store-location strategy around market areas with centrally located distribution centers: Detroit, Kansas City, San Francisco, San Diego, Phoenix, St. Petersburg–Tampa, Houston and Dallas–Fort Worth. Surprisingly, the list did not include the company's Chicago home base. Here, the company took a different approach. Instead of opening new stores, it acquired an existing firm: The Fair, a longtime Chicago department store chain with a flagship on State Street and a few suburban branches.

Initially, the company kept The Fair's name, but conversions began soon. The first Fair store to be converted was at Randhurst Center in 1963. The following year, the Oak Park, Evergreen Plaza and Old Orchard branches also became Montgomery Ward stores.

Finally, in the fall of 1965, the biggest conversion took place with a massive renovation of the enormous State Street store. The company stripped off the 1890s exterior, replacing it with a sleek, modern, arcade-like façade, announcing Montgomery Ward's arrival in downtown Chicago. Customers loved the new locations and especially appreciated the ease of buying Ward's products at well-known store sites. All-new Montgomery Ward stores opened in outlying areas as well, including Dixie Square in Harvard, Illinois (1965), and Yorktown Center in Lombard, Illinois (1967).

In late 1968, Ward's merged with the Container Corporation of America to create a new holding company called Marcor. The following year, Montgomery Ward's annual sales passed the $2 billion mark for the first time. Even catalog sales improved. By the end of the decade, catalog sales were producing almost a quarter of Ward's total sales volume.

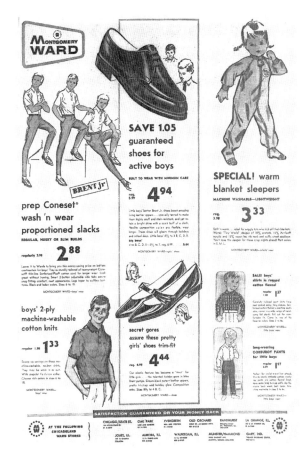

Left: Advertisement, *Chicago Tribune*, November 9, 1964.

Below: Christmas shoppers examine shirts at the Montgomery Ward department store on State Street, 1971. *ST-30004578-0067/*Chicago Sun-Times *collection/ Chicago History Museum.*

Montgomery Ward's 1899 headquarters building at 6 North Michigan Avenue (*left*) contrasted with its 1972 headquarters building at 500 West Superior Street, designed by Minoru Yamasaki. *Left: Detroit Publishing Company/Library of Congress Prints and Photographs Division. Right: Wikimedia Commons/brianhe.*

As the company celebrated its one-hundredth birthday in 1972, officials unveiled plans for a new headquarters building at 500 West Superior Street, just across from the company's historic Chicago Avenue location. Architect Minoru Yamasaki, best known for the World Trade Center in New York City, designed the elegantly understated twenty-six-story skyscraper, which opened in 1974. That same year, Mobil Oil Company acquired a controlling interest in Marcor. By 1980, Montgomery Ward's annual sales of about $5 billion made it the fifth-largest general merchandise retailer in the United States.

But problems still plagued the company. By the late 1970s, its situation had taken a turn for the worse, driven by dismal financial conditions nationally. The company's ongoing attempts to emulate Sears—understandable, given their decades-long competition—proved counterproductive as Sears' own identity problems grew more acute. Competition intensified from specialty stores, big-box stores and the relentless advance of discount stores.

Ward's retail stores by this era seemed to lack a clear niche or strong brand identity. Shoppers in the 1980s still went to Sears for tools, automobile supplies and kitchen appliances and to J.C. Penney for apparel. But for low prices and wide selection, they increasingly chose discount chain stores such as Kmart. "Wards has not established themselves as anything distinctive in the marketplace," explained George Whalin, a retail management consultant, in 2000. "There's just no reason to go there—unless maybe they're the closest store to your home."[89]

The company made various attempts to turn things around, some of which did improve its financial situation, enough that the company was sold to General Electric in 1988. But bad decisions and a sense that the company was a retailing dinosaur still hampered Montgomery Ward.

Even the firm's big general catalog, which sometimes weighed about five pounds and ran to about 1,300 pages, felt dated. "The direction of the catalog business as retailing is specialty catalogs," said Maxwell Sroge, a direct-mail marketing consultant.[90] Mail-order competition became intense in the 1980s, with more than 250 companies involved in catalog operations.

In a move that would have been considered unthinkable a few decades earlier, the company that had invented mail order shut down its general catalog in 1986.

The final demise came slowly. In 1997, Ward's was emerging after being bailed out by General Electric following its second bankruptcy in three years. But even an infusion of cash and remodeled stores could not save the retailer from poor earnings reports. On December 28, 2000, CEO Roger Goddu announced that the company would shut down. "Overall weak holiday sales and a very difficult retail environment simply did not permit us to complete the turnaround that might have been possible in an otherwise thriving economy," Goddu said. "Sadly, today's action is unavoidable."[91] Montgomery Ward's remarkable history, spanning 128 years in American retail, ended in 2001 with the closing of all 250 stores and ten distribution centers.

The legacy of Montgomery Ward remains, however, as a company whose catalogs and stores were cornucopias of dreams and a huge part of many Americans' everyday lives.

"God, it's been here forever," shopper Jeanine Terpening told a PBS reporter at the time of the closing. "This is like losing a best friend. I'm very, very upset about it."[92]

5.

GOLDBLATT'S

The Incredible Bargain Centers

In his 1994 autobiography, *Life Is a Game: Play to Win*, Louis Goldblatt recalled a memorable early Goldblatt Brothers sale, created after his brother Nathan had worked out a good deal on a batch of assorted men's shirts. The shirts hit the sales floor on a particularly busy Saturday. Mixed together, they sat in a big pile on a table whose sign read "Your choice" and listed a single retail price for any one of them.

"On this sale day," explained Louis, "I climbed high on a ladder near the ceiling to open boxes of the shirts, then fling them down on the tables. All the while, I'd shout in English and then in Polish, 'Come and get them. Values to ten dollars. Now on sale; only one dollar. While they last!'"

Customers rushed forward, grabbing for shirts. Louis then whipped up more excitement, tossing a silk shirt into the mix. Having emptied the shelves, he climbed down, picked up shirts that had fallen to the floor, reboxed them and climbed up again. "A new shipment just arrived. Because they are only slightly soiled, here they are, only one dollar each!"[93]

It was exactly the kind of attention-grabbing, excitement-fueled promotional event that made Goldblatt's famous. One of Chicago's longest-lived department stores, Goldblatt's was an innovator that prioritized great prices and energetic promotions.

The Goldblatt's story begins in 1904, when Simon Goldblatt left Stachev, Poland, about one hundred miles from Warsaw, and came to Chicago. He was soon joined by his wife, Hannah, who settled with him and their three oldest sons, Maurice, Louis and Joel, in Chicago's large Polish community.

The couple opened a neighborhood grocery store and butcher shop, with a small apartment in the back for the family, which ultimately included four sons and four daughters. As was common at the time, all the kids helped out in the store almost as soon as they could walk.

Maurice and Nathan struck out on their own in their late teens, taking jobs at a small local department store on Milwaukee Avenue called the Iverson Store. Having learned the ropes and with $500 or so in savings, they decided to go into business for themselves.

In September 1914, Maurice and Nathan opened their first tiny store at 1617 West Chicago Avenue, between Ashland Avenue and Paulina Street. The twenty-four-by-seventy-foot store cost a modest sixty-five dollars a month in rent. Younger brothers Joel, age seven, and Louis, eleven, pitched in on weekends and after school, sweeping the floors and minding the cash register.

From the start, Goldblatt's thrived on innovation. Most stores at the time opened at 9:00 a.m. and closed at 6:00 p.m., leaving little time for working people to shop. So they opened at seven in the morning and stayed open until ten at night.[94] They packed their store with merchandise targeted to the tastes and wallets of immigrants like themselves looking for outstanding bargains on everyday goods.

It worked. In their first year, the Goldblatt brothers made $15,000.[95] Within ten years, they hit sales of $1.4 million. They bought a twenty-five-foot adjoining lot and doubled the size of their store. Finally, in 1923, they put up a three-story structure to house their growing business, now officially called a department store.

Nathan Goldblatt, called Nate, headed up merchandising. He picked up closeouts and irregulars, seeking out bargains regardless of what they were. He once bought a manufacturer's entire inventory of Tingles, a Cracker Jack–like confection. To accommodate that much inventory, the brothers simply tossed aside the crates and boxes they normally used to display merchandise in the store and used cases of Tingles instead.[96]

Nate's tendency to buy over his head led to ongoing quarrels with Maurice, who handled the company's finances and administration, but customers loved the deals. The store was stuffed with goods. Products filled the aisles and spilled onto the sidewalk out front. The brothers pinned blankets, aprons and underwear to the awnings outside, requiring workers to climb ladders on freezing winter nights to retrieve stiff, icy merchandise.

In addition to unbeatable values, Goldblatt's thrived on giant promotions. To advertise a sale of sugar-coated almonds for twenty-six cents a pound, they pasted candied almonds into a heap, labeled "The Snowball Mountain of Sugar-Coated Almonds." The store sold five hundred pounds in one day. A five-foot replica of the Wrigley building, built out of spools of black and white sewing thread, spurred sales of spools of thread by the dozens.[97]

To reach its target market, Goldblatt's advertised not only in the city's *Herald American* and *Daily News* but also in Chicago's foreign-language newspapers for the Polish, Bohemian, German and Jewish communities. The store produced its own advertising circulars, delivered directly to neighborhood residents, an approach many other stores would eventually copy.

When nearby excavation work caused the Goldblatt's building to collapse in 1927, the brothers used the disaster as an opportunity. After staging an impressive sale of salvaged merchandise, they embarked on plans to contract an even larger, grander store than before.[98] The rebuilt store was both bigger and more imposing than most chain and variety stores in Chicago. With its large building and broad selection of merchandise, Goldblatt's now resembled a downtown emporium, but its no-frills interior and emphasis on great values were still pure Goldblatt's.

By 1928, sales had outgrown even the new building, so the brothers began seeking a location for a second store. They purchased the Larkin Company building at Forty-Seventh Street and Ashland Avenue in Back of the Yards, another outlying neighborhood with a mostly working-class immigrant population. Rechristened Goldblatt's, this store succeeded as well. The company's transformation into a full-fledged chain operation had begun.

Goldblatt's rise to national prominence beginning in the late 1920s was nothing short of breathtaking. The brothers typically sought out small department stores in existing Chicago neighborhoods and converted them to Goldblatt's. In 1929, for example, the brothers purchased the Lederer store at Ninety-First Street and Commercial Avenue and the H.C. Struve store at Lincoln and Belmont Avenues. Each was in an established outlying center, easily accessible by mass transportation and already well-populated. This gave Goldblatt's an advantage neither traditional downtown stores nor mail-order retailers had: Goldblatt's stores were located right where their customers were.

By 1930, Goldblatt's had labeled itself "American's Fastest Growing Department Chain," a title it earned by constantly pursuing rapid turnover of goods sold at spectacular prices. Goldblatt's specialized in the types of bargains that discount chain stores would later prioritize: closeouts, irregulars, out-of-season merchandise and goods purchased in large enough volume to ensure maximum discounts from vendors. By paying its vendors quickly and in cash, Goldblatt's often received even bigger discounts.

Goldblatt's store at 1617–25 Chicago Avenue, undated. *Chicago History Museum/ICHi-081625/Raymond W. Trowbridge, photographer.*

"We knew our place in the market and guarded it closely," Louis explained. "We catered to the low-income, blue-collar, working-class family and were able to save them money by maintaining large sales volume per square foot and low expenses."[99] Low expenses meant no carpeting, no elegant fixtures and merchandise jumbled together on the sales floor. Goldblatt's stores had none of the elegant surroundings and pampering customer services now common at the big downtown stores. As historian Richard Longstreth explained, in an era when even Wieboldt's aspired for some of the ambience and services of a big downtown store, "Goldblatt's flaunted cheapness, conspicuously billing its stores as places where immigrants and others with little to spare would find unbeatable bargains."[100]

When the Great Depression hit, Goldblatt's did not just survive, it thrived. Shoppers who a decade earlier might have patronized established full-price department stores now came to Goldblatt's for good deals. Sales nearly tripled between 1931 and 1937. In the early 1930s, the brothers purchased two more city neighborhood stores and three in outlying locations (Hammond, Indiana; Gary, Indiana; and Joliet, Illinois). They also opened a buying office in New York City.

Then, in 1936, the Goldblatt brothers made an unexpected move. They acquired the Davis Store, a lavish, ten-story emporium on Chicago's famed State Street. Goldblatt's was entering the city's high-rent retail district.

The building that Goldblatt's moved into extended for nearly an entire block on State Street between Jackson and Van Buren Streets. Most Chicagoans at the time knew it as the Davis Store, the discount department store run by Marshall Field's since 1923. But the elegant structure had been built for an entirely different department store, A.M. Rothschild and Company.

Rothschild's was one of State Street's largest department stores in the early 1900s, especially after it moved into a new 520,000-square-foot

Postcard view of Rothschild's Department Store, 1916.

structure in 1912. Newspapers heralded the building, with its twenty-foot-wide display windows and two-story-tall arches stretching across the façade as "simple, artistic and dignified."[101] Rothschild's continued until 1923, when company executives sold it to Marshall Field's for $9 million. Field's in turn converted the building to the Davis Store, hoping that a discount store would help Marshall Field's attract budget shoppers.[102] That lasted until 1936.

Acquiring a presence on State Street marked Goldblatt's emergence as a downtown retailer. About four times bigger than any existing Goldblatt's, the State Street store quickly became the firm's flagship. It carried more merchandise—and a fuller range of merchandise—than the neighborhood Goldblatt's stores, as well as more stylish apparel.[103] Just about anything anyone needed could be found there. A July 1936 Circus Day promotion featured curtains, washing machines, kitchen ranges, pots and pans, rugs, garden hose, lawn mowers, chicken feed and even a 118-piece dinner- and glassware set for $27.44.[104] Goldblatt's food department sold not only canned goods but also bakery items, dairy products, fresh produce and meats. One fan later reminisced: "The thing I remember best about Goldblatt's was going to the basement after church on Sunday. The basement was where the food was sold. I remember the strong smell of Polish sausage and to this day whenever I smell Polish sausage, I think 'it smells like Goldblatt's basement.'"[105]

Goldblatt's sales volume soared. The company's overall sales volume in 1935 had been $33 million; by 1937, it reached nearly $50 million, making Goldblatt's second only to Marshall Field's in terms of volume. (Profits declined slightly, although the State Street store held its own.)

With the move to State Street, however, Goldblatt's seemed to falter about its identity. Was it a cost-cutting discounter? Or was it a value-driven but otherwise conventional department store? Should the stores provide spectacular bargains on everyday basic items or discounted versions of what the other major department stores sold? Even the brothers did not always agree.[106]

The growing pains continued throughout the years of World War II. Younger brothers Joel and Louis left for army service, and Nathan Goldblatt developed cancer. After Nathan's death in 1944, Maurice devoted himself to the fight against cancer and heart disease, raising millions for research and treatment.[107]

Still, as the nation emerged from the war, Goldblatt's reorganized and began to grow again, launching an aggressive expansive program.

A typically exuberant Goldblatt's advertisement (partial), *Chicago Tribune*, July 5, 1936.

By 1960, Goldblatt's had twenty stores, most of which were brand-new stores, not conversions of preexisting department stores in established city neighborhoods. Some of the new stores were in Chicago, but six were located in the rapidly expanding suburbs, another four were in outlying Illinois cities and four more were in neighboring states.

Women with full carts wait in line at the Goldblatt's store on State Street during a special food sale, February 1947. *Wallace Kirkland/ The* LIFE *Picture Collection/Shutterstock.*

Many of the company's postwar stores opened in shopping centers, starting in 1953 with the opening of a Goldblatt's in the new planned community of Park Forest, which boasted one of the nation's first outdoor shopping centers. Two years later, in 1955, a Goldblatt's opened in the Scottsdale shopping center on the southwest side of Chicago. Three more debuted in 1956, followed by two in 1958 and two in 1959, all in shopping centers.

Strategically, these shopping centers were not major regional shopping malls, but medium- and small-sized shopping centers. While not as glamorous or expansive as the major malls, the smaller centers targeted populations not served by those larger malls and allowed Goldblatt's to dominate new retail expansion in each location.[108]

As far as customers were concerned, Goldblatt's remained the place to go for fun-filled promotional events—and great prices, encapsulated in the company's slogan "the incredible bargain centers."

In an era when most department stores still kept merchandise behind the counters, Goldblatt's piled its products onto tables where customers could see and handle them.[109] This often created clutter, but as Louis Goldblatt explained it, "Goldblatt's was a beehive of excitement and fun; it was not intended to be fancy or even comfortable."[110] Self-service and no-frills interiors, combined with shrewd buying of discounted goods, kept Goldblatt's

A Goldblatt's store in April 1951, shown prior to its grand opening—and then packed with shoppers. *Francis Miller/The* LIFE *Collection/Shutterstock.*

Cattle paraded on State Street in front of the Goldblatt's store as part of a company food sale promotion in February 1947. *Wallace Kirkland/The* LIFE *Picture Collection/Shutterstock.*

prices low, as did its continued emphasis on volume selling. Families living on tight budgets loved Goldblatt's, but so did anyone who prized a great deal, including celebrities.

And what the stores lacked in amenities they made up for in an expansive variety of merchandise. Company advertisements in 1961 offered just about anything a customer might want: mattresses, ballpoint pens, jewelry boxes, sectional sofas, gift wrap, typewriters and canaries guaranteed to sing. You could buy a portable television for $199.95 or a green turtle for $0.29.

On the surface, it appeared that Goldblatt's was on an unstoppable path of growth. At a 1954 luncheon celebrating the company's fortieth

Gospel singer Mahalia Jackson shopping at Goldblatt's on State Street, August 1963. *ST-19130507-0008/*Chicago Sun-Times *collection/Chicago History Museum.*

anniversary, Joel Goldblatt predicted that over the next twenty years, the firm would double its volume of business, stating, "There is every possibility that Goldblatt's, using Chicago as a core, will have many stores in other cities within a 200 mile radius."[111]

Still, starting with the move to State Street, Goldblatt's seemed less an innovator and more a conventional department store. For all the undeniable growth, the company's new stores in the postwar era failed to bring in the profits of earlier decades. Although sales rose from $48 million to $108 million between 1940 and 1960, the increases now came more slowly, and profits began to decline. The company posted its first ever loss in 1963. By the 1960s, Goldblatt's had increasingly become known not for its innovations but for its cheapness and its lesser standing compared to other Chicago department stores.

With the benefit of hindsight, some commentators have speculated that Goldblatt's failed to adjust its merchandise to fit the tastes of middle-class customers of its outlying stores and even the rising incomes of blue-collar families in the postwar era. Company executives also seemed slow to adjust to the demands of operating a large-scale regional company the way Sears did. Discount stores such as Zayre, Venture, Turn Style and

Kmart, which emerged as strong competition in the 1960s, cut heavily into Goldblatt's revenues.

Constant family bickering did not help. Goldblatt family members, who still dominated executive positions, rarely agreed on company strategy—or anything. An executive who worked under three different chief executives in less than two years in the 1970s said: "Every time two of them got together, they threw the third one out. I've never seen such spite voting on a board of directors."[112]

The company's operations crested in the 1970s, when Goldblatt's had forty-seven stores and close to $250 million in annual sales, but it was losing steam as it continued to battle ever-growing competition, shifting customer needs and out-of-date stores. Longstreth summed up the feeling of many when he said, "Ultimately, Goldblatt's became known more for its shortcomings than its earlier successes."[113]

In 1981, Goldblatt's declared bankruptcy. It reemerged in the mid-1980s as a streamlined operation with about fifteen stores, mostly targeting the same budget-minded, immigrant and working-class customers Goldblatt's had served from the beginning. The flagship store on State Street closed, later to be remodeled by DePaul University as part of its Loop campus. But Goldblatt's never really hit its stride again. In 2003, with only six stores left, the company liquidated.

Goldblatt's pioneered some of the innovative merchandising and sales approaches that would later be taken up by the national discount chains. Its

The Goldblatt's store in the Green Meadows Shopping Center, Addison, which opened in 1962 (seen here in 1976). *Joe Archie.*

bargain prices earned it loyal customers, as did its convenient locations and responsiveness to local consumer needs. Shoppers fondly recall Goldblatt's noisy basement pet departments and the enticing smell of food from the deli and snack departments. Customer Shirley Walker said, "I remember walking down Ashland Avenue and visiting the 47th and Ashland Goldblatt's store. My mom used to purchase her canaries there. I remember getting 6 finches there for around $2 each."[114]

Shoppers reminisce about Goldblatt's much-loved sidewalk sales, the big metal root beer dispensers, the store's delicious boiled ham and its trademark cheesecake. More than anything, they remember a store that promised outstanding bargains—and you didn't have to travel far to get them.

6.

WIEBOLDT'S

Where You Buy with Confidence

Chicagoans rummaging for clothing bargains in the T.J. Maxx or Burlington stores at 1 North State Street today might, if they have a long memory, remember the building as home to Wieboldt's. The building housed Wieboldt Stores' flagship store from 1960 to 1987.

Not many, however, will remember it as Mandel Brothers, the department store that not only built the structure in 1912 but was also one of Chicago's pioneer department stores. Although largely forgotten today, Mandel Brothers once ranked among Chicago's largest and busiest department store companies, with a history that reads like a rags-to-riches Horatio Alger story.

The Mandel name first appears in Chicago retail history in 1855. That year, Bavarian immigrants Solomon Mandel and his uncle Simon Klein organized a partnership called Klein and Mandel to run a dry-goods business on Clark Street. It became Mandel Brothers after Solomon's three brothers, Leon, Simon and Emanuel, came in and Klein departed.

When the brothers' store at State and Harrison Streets was wiped out in the Great Chicago Fire of 1871, they built a larger store on the same site. That store burned in 1874, marking two times in three years that the Mandels lost everything to fire.

Undeterred, the brothers again reestablished themselves. They reopened in a new location at 121–23 State Street at the urging of Marshall Field himself. "We welcome competition," Field explained. "It will bring more customers to State Street and we'll undertake to get our share of the business."[115]

Postcard view of the Mandel Brothers store at 1 North State Street, captioned "State and Madison Streets, 'Busiest Corner in the World.'" Circa 1923.

Mandel Brothers flourished on State Street, so much that in the 1880s and 1890s, it expanded by purchasing or leasing several adjacent buildings. By the 1880s, the firm employed more than eight hundred people. By the early 1900s, it employed more than three thousand.

And the Mandel family was not done yet. A second generation of Mandels now rose to leadership. After acquiring a lease for the northeast corner of Madison Street and Wabash Avenue in 1900, the company embarked on a project to replace all of its State Street frontage with a massive new sixteen-story structure. The strikingly modern building, opened in 1912, included a first floor paved in marble and finished with mahogany wood, a private telephone exchange larger than some small towns, thirty hydraulic elevators and three sets of escalators. Store executives boasted that it was 450 times the size of the founders' original 1855 store.[116]

Sales slumped during the Great Depression (annual sales dipped to under $15 million in 1931), but the company persevered. In 1934, Mandel Brothers, then the largest Jewish-owned department store outside of New York City, created a sensation when General Manager Leon Mandel announced that the store had discontinued all purchases of German productions owing to customer resistance.[117] With that, it became one of the first American retailers to oppose Nazi leader and German dictator Adolf Hitler.

After World War II, Mandel Brothers spent more than $2 million to modernize the store, putting in a new air-conditioning system, along with new escalators. That promising rebound soon stalled, however. As shopping areas in outlying areas drained customers from downtown, the firm seemed reluctant to expand. Executives opened only one branch store, in the Lincoln Village Shopping Center at Lincoln Avenue and McCormick Road, which opened in 1952. On opening day, a crowd of 2,200 customers poured in during the first thirty minutes.[118]

Unfortunately, the new branch did not herald new growth. The company opened no additional branches, as business began to plummet. Annual sales revenue dropped 19 percent between 1948 and 1958. Between 1952 and 1960, Mandel Brothers posted a profit only twice.[119] Analysts speculate that Mandel's remained committed only to its downtown store until it had lost too much market share to compete.

It was a sad reversal of fortune for a business that celebrated its one-hundredth anniversary in 1955 with family members still in top executive positions. As the decline accelerated, store executives began looking for a buyer. After lengthy discussions, Wieboldt's purchased Mandel Brothers for $2.75 million and stock transfers in August 1960.[120]

Interior view of Mandel Brothers department store, circa 1950s. Signs on the columns read "Air Conditioning Keeps Mandel's Cool as a Lake Breeze." *Chicago History Museum/ Getty Images.*

With that, the name *Mandel Brothers* disappeared from storefronts. Wieboldt's acquired not only the company but also its prime location at State and Madison Streets.

It must have looked like an obvious move to many. State Street in 1960 retained its reputation at the city's most important retail corridor. James Tobin, then president of Wieboldt's, said, "Entering State street is an obvious move in our expansion program."[121]

Not everyone, however, wanted to shop there. Ethnic, class and racial differences caused many Chicagoans to avoid State Street altogether. Many workers did not reach a standard of living to enter the consumer class until after World War II or later. Racial discrimination and language barriers kept many African American and non-English-speaking immigrant customers out of some stores.[122]

Not surprisingly, then, as Chicago's population grew and the city expanded outward, small neighborhood shopping districts emerged. Often located where public transportation lines intersected, stores in these areas were smaller than the downtown emporia but much more convenient. They catered to working-class and minority customers who did not care to travel downtown.

This is where William A. Wieboldt carved out his niche. Born in 1857 in Altenbruch, Germany, Wieboldt came to Chicago at the age of fourteen, just in time to witness the Great Chicago Fire of 1871. A letter he wrote home to his parents in Germany reveals his growing love for his new hometown: "[Three-quarters] of the lovely, beautiful, yes magnificent city of Chicago burned down in less than 24 hours….Oh, it looks terrible and especially because the beautiful proudest section of the city where the large buildings such as are not to be seen in Germany, and which you can hardly imagine, were destroyed."[123]

Undaunted by the destruction, he stayed, working for twelve years at a general merchandise store on Blue Island Avenue. He married fellow German immigrant Anna Louisa Kruger in 1883 and, one week after their wedding, used his $2,600 savings to open a small general store on the Near North Side with his wife as partner.[124]

One year later, he moved to a new location on Milwaukee Avenue near Ashland Avenue in a densely populated blue-collar neighborhood on Chicago's Northwest Side. His store featured unpretentious merchandise and a multilingual staff to serve immigrant residents in the surrounding area.

Wieboldt's vision, from the start, was to be a neighborhood store, not a downtown behemoth. He keyed his merchandise to serve the needs of

Postcard view of the W.A. Wieboldt store, Milwaukee Avenue and Paulina Street. Undated.

immigrants and the working poor. In the words of one biographer, he "preferred the friendship of the 'little people' and rarely was seen in what is called 'high society.'"[125] Wieboldt's advertisements in the independent Polish-language newspaper *Dziennik Chicagoski* far outnumbered its ads in the *Chicago Tribune* or *Inter Ocean*. An obituary after his death quoted Wieboldt as saying: "My heart is in the neighborhood store. Then I'm part of the community."[126]

It was a winning formula. The original Wieboldt's store expanded over the years, eventually becoming nearly as large as some State Street stores. By the 1910s, Wieboldt's employed some seven hundred people and brought in about $3 million in annual sales.

Then, in 1917, the firm embarked on a new path. It opened a second department store, between Lincoln and Ashland Avenues, just north of Belmont. Actually, William Wieboldt's original idea, when he financed a small retail business called G. Linning and Company in the neighborhood, was that in time his son Elmer would run it. His other son, Werner, would run the Milwaukee Avenue store.

The brothers had other ideas. Convinced that there were advantages in running both stores as Wieboldt's, they put Wieboldt's signs on the Linning store.[127] With that, Wieboldt's took its first steps toward becoming a chain. Located at a significant streetcar transfer point, the substantial new store featured seven floors of merchandise. In 1924, a two-story annex opened across School Street, connected by a basement to the larger building.

Then, in 1925, a third store opened on the city's West Side, on Adams Street between Ashland and Ogden Avenues. Another spacious building, this store was designed by the celebrated architecture firm Graham, Anderson, Probst & White.

The Wieboldt sons largely spearheaded this new direction for the company. William A. Wieboldt retired from active management in 1923, declaring that he and Anna wanted to return to the Chicago area much of the wealth they had amassed in it. They used $5 million to start the Wieboldt Foundation, offering support to "charities designed to put an end to the need for charity."[128]

As a retailer, Wieboldt's was emerging as something new for Chicago: a department store chain with locations in large, well-established neighborhood shopping districts on the outskirts of the city. Its stores, all medium-sized and featuring merchandise at good value, served prosperous blue-collar and budget-conscious middle-class customers. The stores were big enough to feature large assortments of merchandise and some of the

Customers shop in the Wieboldt's store at Ashland and Monroe Streets in 1925. *Kaufmann & Fabry/Centennial Business Collection/Abraham Lincoln Presidential Library and Museum.*

elegant trimmings of a big downtown store, and the locations were easily reached by elevated railroad and streetcar lines, as well as by automobile. The company advanced, in the words of Richard Longstreth, "the idea that upwardly mobile immigrants could have a grand emporium in their own precinct."[129]

In 1929, Wieboldt's purchased an existing department store in Evanston called Rosenberg's and transformed it into the fourth Wieboldt's. Improvements in transportation meant that by the 1920s, Evanston was less isolated from downtown than it had been. Better transportation and increased advertising from downtown department stores put a squeeze on smaller stores like Rosenberg's.[130] Wieboldt's promised it would give North Shore residents "the advantages to be had from being part of a $25,000,000 volume organization," to be visible in "notable savings."[131]

Even as the company was opening in Evanston, it broke ground for a fifth branch store in the Englewood neighborhood on Chicago's South Side. Located at Sixty-Third and Green Streets, just one block west of Englewood's busy Halsted Street commercial district, this Wieboldt's opened in September 1930.

With the opening of the Englewood store, Wieboldt's had emerged as a large local chain operation. Its stores offered a wide selection of merchandise and were located in outlying city neighborhoods, near enough to be easily accessible and big enough to leverage buying power into savings for customers.

By 1930, Wieboldt's five stores were bringing in a combined $21 million in sales. The company experienced some setbacks during the Great Depression but rebounded enough by 1937 to make a splashy mark on the world of department store architecture with the opening of a new branch store in River Forest at Harlem Avenue and Lake Street, part of the booming Oak Park/River Forest retail district. Advertised as the largest suburban department store in the nation, it was almost twice the size of Marshall Field's nearby Oak Park branch. Its sleek style, with long horizontal bands of glass blocks running the length of the store's frontage, was aggressively modern. The whole building exuded stylish innovation. With ample parking in its off-street parking lot and air-conditioning throughout, Wieboldt's seemed to herald the shape of things to come.

Wieboldt's enjoyed another growth spurt after World War II. In the fifteen years after the war, the company opened three new stores and acquired a fourth. One of the new stores, a replacement of the branch in Evanston, featured strikingly modern architecture with rounded corners and vast, windowless expanses.

The company, however, seemed less innovative now than it had in the 1920s and 1930s. Wieboldt's kept targeting the same types of customers it always had. The visually dramatic Wieboldt's at Harlem Irving Plaza in Norridge, with its diamond-patterned façade, opened as part of a spacious shopping center serving an already well-established, relatively dense, lower-middle-class residential neighborhood.

Now too large to easily cater to the local needs of shoppers, Wieboldt's stores increasingly emulated the larger downtown department stores, with bargain basements, snack shops and festive window displays at Christmas.

In 1957, Wieboldt's began to issue and redeem Sperry & Hutchinson trading stamps.[132] As the only major department store group in Chicago to offer the wildly popular S&H Green Stamps, Wieboldt's gained instant popularity. All Wieboldt's stores but one eventually had redemption centers, where shoppers could redeem booklets filled with customer-loyalty stamps given out with merchandise purchases. The company would at one point advertise the redemption center on its State Street store's ninth floor as the largest in the world.

Above, left: Wieboldt's advertisement, newspaper unknown, 1951.

Above, right: Entrance to the Wieboldt's store at Harlem Irving Plaza in the Norridge neighborhood, opened in 1957. *HBSN-00360-B/Chicago History Museum/Hedrick-Blessing Collection.*

Right: Advertisement, *Chicago Tribune*, November 18, 1969.

Given the company's longtime avoidance of State Street, the decision to acquire Mandel Brothers in 1960 seemed curious. As late as 1944, Elmer Wieboldt had written, "Whenever I see the throngs barely able to find space on the sidewalks [of State Street], I become envious, until I remember that the trade of these customers is divided among so many stores."[133] Signs already indicated that there were too many stores, and they were too big, to be supported by the number of shoppers on State Street. Given the turnover he had seen among budget-priced stores in the State Street retail corridor, Elmer had long felt the company's decision not to join the big leagues on State Street—to "continue as smaller fishes in smaller ponds"—was one of the best decisions the company ever made.

Wieboldt's at midcentury seemed to be transforming into a more traditional department store chain. Squeezed by the proliferation of competing department stores and ever-growing competition from discount stores, Wieboldt's executives must have found it hard to resist the prestige associated with having a grand downtown building. Quickly converted to the Wieboldt's nameplate, the store became the new flagship of the chain.

So, even as downtown urban locations were on the wane for department store shopping, Wieboldt's joined the lineup of State Street's popular-priced stores that already included Goldblatt's, Sears and The Fair (soon to become part of Montgomery Ward). The company updated the retail floors, although the enormous fifteen-story building, with its vertical layout, was unavoidably outdated by 1960s merchandising standards.

By this era, Wieboldt's popularity rested on its reputation as a store that was more affordable than Marshall Field's but more upscale than discount retailers. It was also a long-standing presence in many Chicagoans' lives. "The store at Ford City was huge and had an abundance of merchandise. It had everything you need," remembered blogger and podcaster Pete Kastanes. "The quality of merchandise when it came to clothes, appliances, jewelry and other items were top-notch."[134]

When Wieboldt's celebrated its one-hundredth birthday in 1983, an advertisement in the *Chicago Sun-Times* proudly proclaimed, "An important part of Chicago's past, we look to the future with confidence and enthusiasm."[135]

It was, perhaps, hopeful thinking. The chain abandoned the S&H Green Stamp program in 1976.[136] The stamps were no longer as popular as they had been, having been hit hard by the recessions of the 1970s and a decline in the value of the rewards. And the firm was now struggling to stay profitable, caught between the cheap merchandise available at discount stores and the luxury merchandise of upscale stores. The Englewood location closed in

Wieboldt's new store at 1 North State Street, circa 1961. *Kirn Vintage Stock/Corbis via Getty Images.*

Customers browse jewelry in the newly remodeled first floor at Wieboldt's State Street store, August 1976. *ST-20003706-0004/*Chicago Sun-Times *collection/Chicago History Museum.*

1975; the Evanston store closed in 1982. Finally, in 1986, Wieboldt's declared bankruptcy, from which it never recovered. By the end of 1987, all Wieboldt's stores had closed, including the State Street flagship. "They put up a valiant struggle," said Sarah Bode, then president of the Greater State Street Council, "but those huge old flagship stores can be just too costly to maintain."[137]

Many Chicagoans still look back fondly on Wieboldt's, remembering it as a great place to find affordably priced luxuries. They remember savoring the store's signature pound cake (sold by the pound) and browsing the large toy department, called the Toyteria. Many teenagers got their first jobs at a Wieboldt's store, and employees loved the generous 20 percent employee discount. Some of the fondest memories involve S&H Green Stamps. "My mom collected S&H Green Stamps and as a special treat, she would let each of us redeem the stamps for a little gift once in a blue moon," said Betsy Weiss Van Die. "I still have a little gold tone heart pendant with fake fire opal that both my younger sister Janet and I got—we must have been about five and nine respectively."[138]

In addition to the memories, the Wieboldt Foundation lives on, still serving the city's neighborhoods, supporting philanthropic projects in education, affordable housing and justice. You can even find Wieboldt family members sitting on the foundation's board.

7.

SEARS, ROEBUCK

Cheapest Supply House on Earth

In early 1925, some Chicagoans must have been surprised to see a newspaper advertisement from Sears, Roebuck and Company, the nation's leading mail-order firm. Sears, the advertisement announced, would soon open a retail store at its sprawling headquarters on the city's West Side.[139]

That Sears would be growing surprised no one. The company had already outgrown several Chicago buildings and shown a flair for innovation that was nothing short of spectacular. Since its founding some forty years earlier, however, Sears had been exclusively a mail-order operation. Now it would be running, for the first time in its history, a brick-and-mortar department store.

Nothing suggested that a young railroad clerk in rural Minnesota named Richard Sears had a department store in mind when he launched his small watch company in 1886. A local jeweler had rejected a consignment of pocket watches, so Sears picked them up and resold them to other station agents at a two-dollar profit. Realizing he had a knack for sales, he grew the business, adding jewelry and eventually bringing in Alvah C. Roebuck as the company's watch repairman.

Sears's initial catalogs contained only watches and jewelry, but the first general merchandise Sears, Roebuck catalog went out in 1893, a thick 507-page book.[140] Montgomery Ward's catalog had been around since the 1870s, but Sears quickly surpassed it, achieving $10 million in annual sales by 1900, when Ward's stood at $8.7 million.

Richard W. Sears, seated at his desk, from a set of stereoscope views produced by Sears, circa 1906.

Richard Sears himself wrote the catalog text, extolling his products to rural customers who lived far from the big department stores of American cities. He relished the hard sell, prompting one colleague to quip, "He could probably sell a breath of air."[141] The catalogs offered farmers and small-town residents a dizzying cornucopia of items—far more than their hometown general stores ever could—at fabulously low prices. A wide selection of merchandise, low prices and zingy descriptions shot the Sears catalog into mind-boggling popularity.

Sears delighted in extravagant description, but he also stood behind his goods. The catalog invited consumers to "send no money" for big-ticket items such as wood stoves, organs and bicycles. The company would ship an item to your nearest freight depot. You only paid if you found the item "perfectly satisfactory, exactly as represented." The offer built trust and converted many skeptical shoppers into buyers.

Like the Montgomery Ward catalog, the Sears catalog capitalized on the nation's expanding rail system and postal innovations like rural free delivery and parcel post that made delivery of catalogs and merchandise significantly easier. With its business prospering, Sears moved to an expansive forty-acre campus in 1906 on the city's West Side. The new headquarters, at Homan Avenue and Arthington Street, included a printing plant, a powerhouse, landscaped parks and a gigantic U-shaped merchandise building that

Advertisement for the Superba washing machine, from the 1908 *Sears, Roebuck and Co. Catalogue*.

incorporated railroad tracks into its design. A tall tower, topped with the words *Sears Roebuck and Co.* (and hiding a water tank) soon became a Chicago landmark. Sears' mail-order "city" would serve as the company's headquarters for the next sixty-seven years.[142]

When Richard Sears resigned in 1908, pioneering retailer Julius Rosenwald, who had joined the company as a partner in 1895, took over as president and led Sears to even greater heights. Mail-order sales rose sixfold between 1908 and 1911, leaving Rosenwald with a personal fortune that enabled him to become a prominent philanthropist. Customers bought everything for their houses from Sears—including the house itself. Between 1908 and 1940, Sears sold kit homes. Prices in the 1930s ranged from $869 to $3,189 (about $16,600 to $61,100 in today's money).[143] Chicago-area kit house researcher Lara Solonicke explains, "Sears sold affordable houses in their catalog, and that gave all Americans—including women, minorities and immigrants—the chance to become homeowners."[144]

By the late 1910s, however, mail order was shrinking as the automobile shifted America's shopping habits, and Rosenwald believed new management could help Sears respond. The man to do it turned out to be Robert E. Wood, an energetic former military man with a love for studying demographics. Hired away from rival Montgomery Ward, Wood served first as vice-president and later president and board chairman.[145] He got to work, starting with an increase in the company's promotion of automobile products. One line of tires got the name *Allstate*.

Still, the opening of the first Sears retail store on February 2, 1925, took many by surprise. Although in many ways just an extension of its mail-order operations, it marked a distinct turn for the company. In fact, Sears' first store seemed to break all the rules for a large retail emporium. It was located five miles from the city's primary retail corridor on State Street, forcing nonlocals to make a special trip. Prices were slightly higher than those in the catalog (to cover overhead). Perhaps most surprisingly, it catered just as heavily to men as it did to women, with tires, paint, monkey wrenches and auto tents prominently featured alongside women's velvet-trimmed hats and cotton blouses. The store itself had no fancy architecture or pampering customer services other than an optical shop and a soda fountain. Payment was strictly in cash.[146]

The approach worked. By the end of that year, Sears had opened seven more retail stores around the country, four of them in existing mail-order plants.[147]

After that, Sears opened retail stores at an astonishing pace. Within five years, Sears could boast more than three hundred stores, ranging in size from large A stores to medium-sized B stores and small C stores. During one hectic stretch in the late 1920s, Sears opened, on average, one store every other business day.[148]

The majority of these were small stores. By 1934, nearly one in four Sears stores was the smaller C type, located on main streets in city suburbs. These stores did not stock apparel but catered to homeowners with hard goods, including paint, lawn mowers, automobile supplies, sporting goods and hardware.[149]

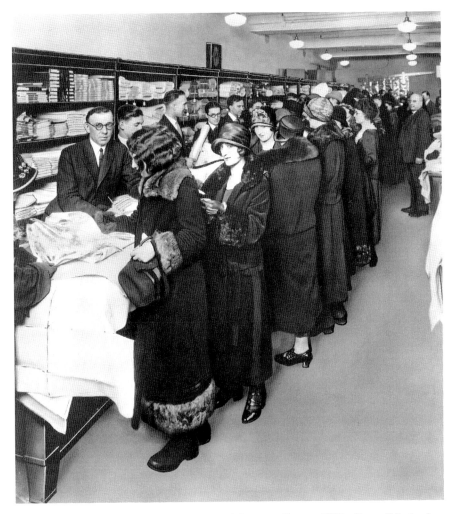

Shoppers crowd the counter at a newly opened Sears retail store, 1920s. *Everett Collection/ Shutterstock.*

The company had reinvented shopping for the second time, correctly predicting that small-town and suburban shoppers were no longer limited to mail order. As Americans continued giving up farms for factories and the nation's population kept shifting to cities and towns, Sears wanted to be there first. When Wood assumed the presidency in 1928, he moved aggressively, ordering a sixfold increase in retail stores. By 1929, retail sales made up half the company's total volume. By 1931, retail store sales topped mail-order sales.

Sears store at 170 North York Street, Elmhurst. This store opened around 1937 and closed in the mid-1960s after Sears opened a store in nearby Oakbrook Center. *Photograph courtesy of Elmhurst History Museum.*

Clearly, Sears' vision for a department store worked. Unlike congested downtown retail corridors, the locations of Sears' stores had plenty of space for free parking. Sears took advantage of inexpensive tracts of land to sprawl horizontally, a thrifty decision, as horizontal buildings cost less to construct. Many included a tower, useful both to conceal a rooftop water tank and as a "beacon to motorists."[150]

Sears continued to build on its reputation for helpfulness and dependability. It procured a radio station license in 1923 (sold in 1935) that would eventually receive the call letters WLS, for World's Largest Store.[151] The station broadcast helpful market reports for farmers, storm warnings and the popular Saturday night *National Barn Dance*. In 1927, Sears acquired the name *Craftsman* for its line of power tools and lawn mowers, joined the same year by *Kenmore* for home appliances.

In 1932, Sears took another bold step, opening a big A store on State Street. It would be the firm's first store in a major downtown shopping district. The structure, known as the Second Leiter Building, stood on

State Street between Van Buren and Congress Streets. Formerly home to the Siegel, Cooper discount department store, it rose eight stories and stretched an entire block, with a 402-foot-long façade. Designed by William Le Baron Jenney in 1891, it featured a façade of smooth white granite arranged into a large, window-filled grid, with minimal exterior ornamentation. As historian Donald Miller explained, its significance lies in how well its art mirrors its engineering: "Jenney's supreme achievement, it is one of the most original and impressive works of modern American architecture, a true cathedral of commerce."[152]

Sears spent thousands of dollars sprucing up the store, which drew fifteen thousand shoppers on its first day and required more than one thousand employees to staff it.[153] City customers who had wisecracked about "Shears, Sawbuck" now snapped up the same automobile supplies, gardening tools, rugs, baby carriages and curtains that rural shoppers had appreciated for years.

By the 1930s, Sears had become the nation's biggest seller of power tools and the third-largest seller of electric refrigerators. In just about a decade,

Postcard view of Siegel, Cooper's State Street store, circa 1907.

Robert E. Wood had transformed Sears from a mail-order business into a national store operation as well.

Remarkably, Sears' department stores coexisted peacefully with the mail-order catalog. The fall catalog in 1933 contained an awe-inspiring 1,060 pages. That same year, Sears' legendary catalog of Christmas gift ideas— renamed the Wish Book in 1968—launched as a separate catalog. "We take it for granted now, but it was truly world-changing at the time to have so many different products, 600 pages worth, at our fingertips," said Jason Liebig, founder of WishBookWeb, a website dedicated to vintage Christmas catalogs.[154] Sears' Christmas catalog changed holiday shopping, making it possible for busy shoppers to buy everything a loved one wanted for Christmas, even if they lived far from a Sears store.

Sears continued to innovate in department store architecture. It acquired an earlier chain of department stores, Becker-Ryan, and in 1933 tore down the old Becker-Ryan store at Sixty-Third and Halsted Streets in Chicago's Englewood neighborhood and built the first nearly windowless department store. Inspired by architecture seen at Chicago's recent Century of Progress Exposition, the building flew in the face of traditional department store design, which had long prioritized windows for daylight and ventilation. New advances in fluorescent lighting and air-cooling, Sears argued, made windows unnecessary. Solid walls sealed out noise and grime while permitting easy temperature control. The bold look positioned the company as a progressive establishment, and Sears soon covered up the windows in many of its older stores.[155]

The opening of a new Sears store always created excitement. An estimated one hundred thousand people visited the Sears at the Six Corners intersection of Irving Park Road and Milwaukee and Cicero Avenues in the Portage Park neighborhood on the day it opened in 1938. The gigantic solid-walled building cost $1 million to erect and featured what was then the largest display window in the city.[156]

World War II temporarily stopped Sears' retail expansion, but as the war's end approached, Wood moved ahead again, telling his staff, "This is no time to stand still!" He ordered the acquisition of property for future new sites around the country. His conviction that pent-up demand for consumer goods would mean a postwar boom proved correct. By the end of 1947, Sears could boast 625 stores scattered across forty-seven states, not to mention another 40 new catalog stores to support telephone sales. "While Montgomery Ward, under dogmatic Sewell Avery, chose to conserve cash (building not a single new store between 1941 and 1958), in

The Sears store facing Halsted Street in the Englewood business district, circa 1976. *Lynette Miller*/Chicago Tribune *Archive Photos/TCA.*

Sears store at the Golf Mill Shopping Center in Niles, March 14, 1964. *John Vogele/* Chicago Tribune.

just three postwar years, Sears sales doubled to twice that of its arch rival," said author Lorin Sorensen.[157]

Sears was not just prospering, it was booming. Unlike most American department stores, Sears aimed for a national store presence, just as it had with its catalog. Sears stores had a clear identity: low prices, extraordinary selection and good quality. Shoppers knew the company's apparel would be more utilitarian and durable than hip and trendy. Its freezers, automatic washers and television sets could be repaired with no problems by Sears' servicemen, who drove trucks with the familiar swooping Sears logo. Sears stores had minimal decor and catered to customers looking for practical items at good prices.

Rapid and aggressive growth slowed in the early 1950s, but Sears showed no signs of stopping. The company increasingly faced competition from both specialty shops and discount chain stores, but it still sold nearly three times more merchandise than its nearest competitor, J.C. Penney. Sears' brand names, like J.C. Higgins sports equipment, Homart plumbing supplies and Tower cameras, were now as familiar to middle-class American families as Kenmore and Craftsman.

The company celebrated its seventy-fifth diamond jubilee in 1961, still showing an uncanny ability to adapt to changing consumer needs. When enclosed shopping malls started going up in the 1960s, Sears stores anchored many of them. As the company's target middle-class shopper grew more affluent, Sears began sprucing up its merchandise, offering mink coats and signing on actor and art aficionado Vincent Price to choose original fine art to be sold in stores across the country.[158]

BusinessWeek magazine reported in January 1968: "What is most impressive about Sears is that a company of this size can be so quick on its feet. It was the first to move to the suburbs; it pushed credit when J.C. Penney was sticking to a cash-only policy, it pioneered in self-selection, night hours, telephone shopping."[159]

For Chicagoans, Sears in the 1960s and 1970s had become an enormous part of everyday life. Many went to Sears for everything from Kenmore washing machines and DieHard batteries to Toughskins jeans. At Christmas, families went to see the toy display in the large window at State and Van Buren Streets and ride the monorail train in the toy department. When the annual Christmas Wish Book arrived, it sucked children in for weeks.

Mike Lord, who grew up near the Six Corners Sears, remembered sneaking over to the store's television department to watch Cubs games when his parents pushed him to turn off the television and get outside. "It was my babysitter when I couldn't get my friends together to play ball," he said.[160]

Another customer, Lara Lord, remembered Sears stores as one of the few consistent places in an unstable childhood: "Sears throughout the decades was someplace that allowed my working-class, single mom to provide me a decent childhood. My white and gold French Provincial canopy bedroom set was from Sears. It took her a few years to get all the pieces I had, but between their credit line and all, she could provide me with a nice bedroom set."[161] Later, Lord went to Sears for car repairs and new tires, because the company's credit plan, with its reasonable interest rates, helped her afford the upkeep.

Sears in 1969 was so dominant that its sales represented 1 percent of the entire U.S. economy. Two-thirds of Americans shopped there.[162] When Sears moved its headquarters to the newly built 110-story Sears Tower in downtown Chicago in 1973, it was the world's tallest building.

Still, the middle-class, homeowning American families served by Sears hit new challenges in the 1970s, pummeled by recession, inflation and a plunging

The manager of the floor-coverings department shows a carpet sample to a customer in the Golf Mill Sears store, 1961. *AP Photo.*

birth rate. Postwar families who had outfitted their households from Sears no longer bought as much. Financially, the company's performance was flat through the mid-1970s.

Edward Telling, who took the helm in 1978, shook things up. Buying and merchandising operations were centralized, and the company undertook a major corporate reorganization. Some two hundred smaller and older stores were closed, including the very first Sears retail store, which joined the casualty list in 1984. A facelift to Sears' remaining retail stores resulted in interiors that felt fresher and more up-to-date.

In 1984, when Sears boasted more than 800 retail stores and 2,389 catalog-sales centers, *Time* magazine marveled: "The most intriguing thing about Sears is that so many Americans buy so many things there. Sears is a fixture of Americana, like baseball, the Rotary Club or the Boy Scouts."[163]

Still, Sears' identity no longer seemed easy to define. Customers rebuffed higher-priced, more stylish merchandise if it bore the Sears name. When Americans' shopping habits began shifting to stand-alone big-box stores, Sears found it hard to pivot, having invested heavily in shopping mall locations. Walmart, established in 1962, had gone after the discount retail market aggressively, luring away many Sears customers. Shoppers would still visit Sears for major appliances but now went to discounters for things like small appliances and housewares. The company seemed to have lost its retail roots, now offering a range of financial services, including insurance (Allstate), stocks (Dean Witter), real estate (Coldwell Banker) and credit cards (Discover card).

Sears' challenges extended to racial and gender issues as well, as it struggled to adapt to broader national trends. During the Jim Crow era, the Sears catalog had enabled African American families to bypass the humiliations that came with shopping in segregated stores. In the early 1950s, Sears even sold the first mass-produced realistic Black doll.[164] But the company resisted integrating its sales, clerical and managerial jobs for years and firmly opposed organized labor. Lawsuits filed by the Equal Employment Opportunity Commission exposed entrenched racial and gender inequalities at Sears.[165]

In one of the great ironies of retail history, a company that had historically been adept at anticipating shifts in shopping habits now languished. One observer described Sears as caught between high-end and low-end shopping: "Sears [found] itself like a blade of grass trampled on by the elephants at both ends of the bifurcated retail market."[166]

In 1991, Sears fell from its position atop American retail when Walmart surpassed it in total sales revenue. Two years later, in 1993, the company announced the demise of its catalog. "To see it die gives you a little, well, your heart skips a beat because it was something that was so American," said Robert F. Delay, editor of the direct-marketing *DeLay Newsletter.* "Nonetheless, the world has changed, the catalog has not changed with it."[167]

"I think we bought a washing machine from Sears in 2005. Before that, the last thing I bought at Sears was probably a pair of Toughskins jeans (husky!) in the 1970s," remembered Ron Dreher. "I'd guess that our family shopped at Sears at least until the early 1980s. I don't know what happened. Suddenly…we didn't. Like most of America, it seems."[168]

Sears fought to turn things around. The company moved its headquarters to suburban Hoffman Estates, cut the cord with some financial services

Members of the National Organization for Women picket outside the Sears store on State Street on March 27, 1974. *ST-90004388-0011/*Chicago Sun-Times *collection/ Chicago History Museum.*

and opened a new flagship-caliber store at State and Madison Streets, in the former home of The Boston Store. Starting in 1998, the company invited customers to "see the softer side of Sears," in a popular advertising campaign spotlighting the company's apparel. A few years later, the company acquired clothing and home decor retailer Lands' End.

Some of the transformation efforts in the 1990s and early 2000s showed promise, but none gained traction. "Kenmore-branded appliances and the Lands' End stuff are probably still OK, but not that special compared to competitors," said Les Mikesell, who remembered stores with limited cashiers, long lines and aggressive pitches for store loyalty programs.[169] Other shoppers agreed, remembering the stores in this era as tired and outdated, with a generally morose feeling. Even the expansive, well-stocked State Street store did not stand out. "The new store was clean, bright, spacious, and stocked with practical merchandise and helpful sales associates. But the business model was outdated and *there was nothing here to make the shopping experience special*," said historian Eric Bronsky (italics in original).[170]

Many felt hopeful after investor Edward Lampert led Sears through a merger with Kmart in 2004. The newly created Sears Holdings Corporation began shuttering Sears stores nationwide in the 2010s, including stores in Orland Park, Park Forest, Calumet City and Joliet. The flagship store on State Street lasted thirteen years, hemorrhaging millions, before closing in 2014.

For many, the real ending began when Sears Holdings filed for Chapter 11 bankruptcy protection in 2018. That same year, the last Sears within the Chicago city limits, the famous Six Corners Sears in Portage Park, closed just two months shy of its eightieth anniversary. The Chicago Ridge Mall Sears, one of the last full-line Sears stores in the greater Chicago area, closed in February 2021. With that, only one Sears store remained in Illinois, the Woodfield Mall location in suburban Schaumburg. That store shut its doors on November 14, 2021.

Nostalgia permeates many peoples' memories of shopping at Sears. "I used to love going to Sears, going way back to the 1960s when the local store made fresh pretzels near the door, guaranteeing that all kids would demand their mom or dad would take them inside whenever they were in the neighborhood," remembered Steve Corbyn, whose father instilled in him a respect for durable Craftsman tools. "[I]f your socket wrench broke, you just took it to Sears and got a replacement—no questions asked."[171]

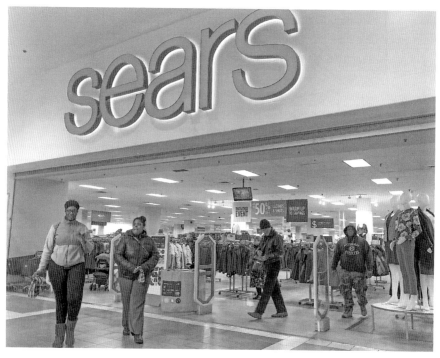

Above: The Sears store at North Riverside Park Mall on December 28, 2018, not long after the company declared bankruptcy. This Sears branch closed in 2020. *Tannen Maury/ EPA-EFE/Shutterstock.*

Left: A customer shops for a Craftsman auto jack at the Sears store in North Riverside Park Mall, 2018. *Tannen Maury/ EPA-EFE/Shutterstock.*

Val Perry Rendel, author of the book *Sears in Chicago*, grew up with parents who met while working for Sears. "Everything in our house—all our linens, dishware, appliances, tools, furnishings and electronics—came from Sears." She bought her daughter a pair of emerald earrings during the clearance sale at the last Sears store in Chicago. "She's still too young for them, but someday I will give them to her and tell her about everything Sears gave to our family and to the city we love, and the legacy it left us."[172]

8.

THE COMPETITION

Specialty and Neighborhood Department Stores

sk someone to name a famous Chicago department store, and you will likely hear the same handful of names: Marshall Field's. Carson Pirie Scott. Sears. Wieboldt's. But the history of Chicago department stores is much larger than this, encompassing hundreds of establishments.

Some of the biggest are barely remembered today. In the 1880s and 1890s, Chicago's booming population spurred the opening of dozens of big stores, many of which began as small dry-goods stores but expanded to become grand, multi-line department stores.

THE BOSTON STORE

The building at the northwest corner of State and Madison Streets looks much the same today as it did in the early twentieth century, when it was home to one of Chicago's largest department stores, The Boston Store. Like many stores, it began as a dry-goods firm, the Pardridge dry-goods store. A young upstart named Charles Netcher joined Pardridge as a cash boy in 1869, worked his way up to partner and then bought out the owners. Grandly renaming his firm The Boston Store (Boston being once synonymous with fashion), he expanded it until it occupied a huge space at State and Madison Streets.

After his death in 1904, Netcher's widow, Mollie, took command, soon transforming the business into a full-line department store and leading it to its greatest success. She oversaw the construction of a magnificent new

The Boston Store, 1929. The view is looking west on Madison Street from State Street. *DN-0087804*/Chicago Sun-Times/Chicago Daily News *collection/Chicago History Museum.*

building, put up in phases between 1905 and 1917. (Later expanded, the building is now known as 1 North Dearborn Street.) At seventeen stories tall, the new Boston Store building had twenty acres of floor space and included a post office station, several restaurants, a first-aid station, a barbershop, a bank and an observation area with spectacular views from 325 feet above the street.[173]

The Boston Store appealed primarily to working-class shoppers, as encapsulated in a popular children's ditty (sung to the tune of the 1890s vaudeville song "Ta-ra-ra Boom-de-ay"):

All the girls who wear high heels,
They trade down at Marshall Field's.
All the girls who scrub the floor,
They trade at the Boston Store.[174]

The Boston Store's popularity peaked in the 1920s. Sales reached almost $33 million in 1922, making The Boston Store the second-highest-grossing department store in Chicago. But the store began faltering during the Great Depression. Mollie Netcher did little over the years to update the store's look—by the 1940s, it "reeked with a quaint Victorian mustiness," said one reporter—or its operations.[175] She showed no interest in opening suburban branches or giving up the store's long-standing cash-only sales policies. The Boston Store finally shuttered in July 1948.

SIEGEL, COOPER

The Boston Store was not the only firm targeting budget shoppers. Equally prominent as a discount department store was Siegel, Cooper and Company. Henry Siegel, Frank H. Cooper and Isaac Keim launched their company in 1887. Just four years later, they moved to a new building at State and Van Buren Streets. Built by Levi Leiter after his split from Marshall Field, the structure known as the Second Leiter building now is recognized as a landmark in Chicago architecture. Everything about the building spoke to its modernity, from its wide-open floors (thanks to the steel-frame skeleton) to its soaring eight-story height. It boasted fifteen acres of floor space and a block-long frontage on State Street.

At the time of the 1893 World's Columbian Exposition, Siegel, Cooper was an enormous retailer with services easily matching those of more high-end stores. Customers could enjoy a comfortable waiting room with free stationery, a café, a children's nursery, a reading room with international newspapers, a dental office, a medical bureau, a barbershop, a savings bank and a "splendidly appointed" restaurant. It confidently called itself "the greatest store in the world."[176]

Siegel, Cooper's future, however, lay in New York City, where the company opened an opulent store in 1896. The Chicago store hung on until 1930, when it closed.

ROTHSCHILD'S

Jewish immigrant Abram M. Rothschild got his big break in 1882, when he married Augusta "Gusta" Morris, daughter of legendary Chicago meat-packer Nelson Morris. The Morris family provided financial backing that allowed Abram to open his own retail clothing company, A.M. Rothschild and Company. It quickly grew into one of the largest retail department stores on State Street. Managing such an enormous store, however, took its toll on Rothschild himself, who proved unequal to the demands. Following some bad business decisions, he stepped down (and later, tragically, committed suicide).

Under the leadership of Gusta Rothschild's father and brothers, the company continued to grow. Store executives cobbled together leases from more than thirty separate business owners to acquire enough land to put up a new structure stretching nearly an entire block along State Street between Jackson and Van Buren Streets. When the new cream-colored building, designed by the renowned architecture firm Holabird and Roche, opened in 1912, newspapers breathlessly described its twenty-foot-wide display windows, revolving entrance doors and two-story arches marching down the façade. Builders had even honored the firm's founder by incorporating the letter R into the building's terra-cotta façade.

Inside, the store boasted twenty-six passenger elevators, a restaurant on the eighth floor with seating for more than one thousand diners, a separate men's restaurant, telephones, a hair salon, a ticket office and fur storage vaults. Merchandise included everything from women's petticoats and shoes to furniture, rugs, groceries and athletic equipment. One might ask, a reporter suggested, "Is there anything you want that you cannot find at Rothschild's?"[177]

Rothschild's remained a significant presence on State Street until 1923, when the heirs of Nelson Morris left the retail business, selling the store to Marshall Field's for $9 million. Field's ran it as a discount department store called The Davis Store for about fifteen years until, during a flurry of operational changes in the mid-1930s, Field's sold it to the Goldblatt brothers. (Gusta, for her part, married another Chicago retailer whose last name also happened to be Rothschild: Maurice L. Rothschild, who operated a large clothing store across the street from the A.M. Rothschild store.)

Specialty Stores

The Boston Store; Siegel, Cooper; and Rothschild's were clearly department stores. Large enterprises, they sold a full line of goods, from clothes and books to housewares, china and furniture. They also used the characteristic form of organization in which each department ran as if it were a separate boutique. The larger entity of "the store" provided things like advertising, cashiering and window displays, but each department had its own budget. Historian Jan Whitaker helpfully suggests that this organizational form distinguishes department stores from specialty stores and older country stores.

Definitions, however, are slippery things. By Whitaker's definition, a large store that sold mostly clothing, such as Lytton's or Chas. A. Stevens, would not qualify. Nor would an appliance and electronics store such as Chicago's legendary Polk Brothers. Yet the customer base for big stores such as Lytton's and Polk Bros. overlapped with stores such as Carson Pirie Scott and Sears. Shoppers seeking a new refrigerator or a cocktail dress rarely made much distinction between a big, multi-line department store and a big appliance or apparel store. When the big department stores began opening smaller shopping-mall stores at midcentury, these branches increasingly resembled specialty clothing stores.

In an even larger sense, Chicago's big specialty stores posed serious competition to the big department stores. Some apparel stores grew so large that they featured an eye-popping number of different departments: suits, shirts, shoes, ties, socks and leather goods for men; dresses, suits, blouses, hats, gloves, hosiery and so on for women. Chicago even had a few specialty clothing stores that were so big they referred to themselves as "department stores." Of these, the biggest were Charles A. Stevens and Henry C. Lytton's The Hub.

Chas. A. Stevens

Charles A. Stevens, or Stevens, as it was familiarly known, started out as a silk specialty firm. Charles Anthony Stevens arrived in Chicago in 1886 from the small town of Colchester, Illinois, where he and his brothers had a dry-goods store. He opened a small silk store on the second floor of a building near Marshall Field's. Legend has it that Stevens was the first in the country to sell ready-made silk blouses and lingerie.[178]

Chas. A. Stevens advertisement, circa 1903.

The idea paid off. Stevens's brothers soon joined him, and the company grew, eventually doing a prosperous mail-order business in women's ready-to-wear apparel. After expanding to several different locations, the firm announced ambitious plans to construct a new store at 17–25 North State Street, between Madison and Washington Streets. The sparkling new terra-cotta tower would have nineteen stories. The lowest floors would house Chas. A. Stevens, while upper floors would contain the best of the city's small specialty retailers. When the building opened in 1912, its arcade passageway extended from State Street to Wabash Avenue and had display windows featuring merchandise from the upstairs tenants—and a bank of elevators ready to whisk you upstairs.

That idea never really took off, but Stevens prospered. By the middle of the twentieth century, the Chas. A. Stevens flagship store was a hub for women's fashion. It included six floors of women's fashions, a restaurant called The Circle and a beauty salon called The Powder Room. In the 1960s, it became the first Chicago retailer to devote a floor to junior fashions, later avowing "many of today's women can recall buying their first mini-skirt at Stevens."[179] Like the big department stores, Stevens moved into the suburbs, opening branch stores in many of Chicago's most-desirable shopping centers. Their convenient locations and fashion expertise drew loyal fans.

"Seemed Stevens always came through when I was in a pinch. A high school dance? They would inevitably have the perfect dress. A new pair of shoes for Easter? Great selection and a beautiful shoe salon. Gift for Mom's birthday? You could find a bottle of a favorite perfume at an affordable price," said Nancy Pipal, who shopped at the La Grange store.[180]

By the 1980s, however, sales had stagnated. In 1986, the company was sold to a group of investors who failed to turn the tide, and in 1988, the 102-year-old company filed for Chapter 11 bankruptcy. "I adored Stevens, and when they went out of business in the 80's, it was personally devastating," said one blogger. "Sure, I liked Marshall Field's, but if I was headed to State Street, it was to shop at Stevens."[181]

LYTTON'S

Farther south on State Street, the retail area near State and Jackson Streets came to be known as home to Chicago's leading men's clothing stores. At midcentury, this is where you would find such apparel stores as Baskin, Bond's, Benson-Rixon and, one of the largest, Lytton's.

Henry C. Lytton and Sons advertisement for two-trouser men's suits at $50 (approximately $798 in today's money), *Chicago Tribune*, April 11, 1924.

Henry C. Lytton, son of a New York shirtmaker, entered the clothing business as an errand boy in 1861. By 1886, he had gained enough experience and saved up enough money to launch a clothing store of his own. He chose Chicago and leased a five-story building at the northwest corner of State and Jackson Streets. When his store opened in 1887, he named it The Hub and proclaimed it the "World's Greatest Clothing Store."

Lytton was, according to one newspaper, "the personification of American gumption, wedded to shrewd showmanship and cultural interest."[182] He quickly became known for his publicity stunts. He once threw overcoats from the roof of his store to the crowd below. He paid off an 1888 election bet on Grover Cleveland by appearing in a display window sawing wood while wearing a tuxedo.[183]

Lytton credited his success to the power of newspaper advertising: "consistent, steady, vigorous advertisement, deftly presented and free from any misrepresentation."[184] Of his initial $12,000 investment, he spent $3,000 on advertising. Chicago's bourgeoning population and The Hub's successful marketing kept it expanding. The store, now calling itself The Hub, Henry C. Lytton and Sons, moved across the street in 1913 to the northeast corner of State and Jackson Streets. The new Lytton's building stood an impressive eighteen stories tall, with The Hub occupying the lower eight floors.

In the 1920s, Lytton's became one of the first major Loop stores to open a branch store in the suburbs. Stores opened in Evanston, Illinois (1926); Gary, Indiana (1926); and Oak Park, Illinois (1927). When the shopping center boom began, Lytton's went along, opening stores in Evergreen Plaza (1952), Golf Mill (1960) and Old Orchard (1965).

Lytton retired in 1917 at the age of 70 but returned to the presidency sixteen years later after his son George died. He remained as president until his death in 1949 at the age of 103. To mark his 100th birthday in 1946, the company officially changed its name to Lytton's (a move that also eased the confusion over other stores called The Hub).[185]

Control of Lytton's passed to a New York men's clothing manufacturer in 1961, but Lytton's suffered in the 1970s from the same shifting apparel-industry economics, financial recession pressures and discount-store competition that hit other clothing retailers. Lytton's was sold again and finally, in March 1984, filed for bankruptcy protection and began closing stores. The firm's owners sold their lease on the flagship State Street store in a last-ditch effort to save the business, but by early 1986, the company's remaining assets were liquidated, and all Lytton's stores shuttered.

Other Specialty Stores

Not all apparel stores were as big as Chas. A. Stevens and Lytton's, but many others were sizeable. Maurice L. Rothschild and Company opened as a small men's apparel store at State and Jackson Streets in 1904 but expanded in 1910 and 1928, becoming an enormous clothing emporium. When the women's apparel store Bramson opened a branch location in Park Forest Plaza in 1958, it included departments for women's clothing, shoes, jewelry, furs and millinery, as well as a beauty salon and a bride's room.[186]

Specialty apparel stores gained a reputation for fashion expertise that often surpassed that of the department stores. Women's apparel stores frequently staged benefit fashion shows for women's clubs and other philanthropic organizations. College board programs, where local college students

A model shows off a dress at a Bramson store, 1952. *Francis Miller/The* LIFE *Picture Collection/Shutterstock.*

acted as fashion advisors to college-age shoppers and received training on merchandising and modeling, helped draw young customers. Marshall Field's, Carson Pirie Scott, The Fair and Wieboldt's had college boards, but so did Chas. A. Stevens, Maurice L. Rothschild, Hirsch Clothing, Lytton's, Bramson, Gilmore and Baskin.

POLK BROS.

If specialty apparel stores gave the department stores a run for their money in fashion, Polk Brothers did the same in appliances and electronics.

Sol Polk, founder of Polk Bros., gained the nickname "master merchandiser" for his innovative merchandising and zany promotions.[187] A showman at heart, he and his brother Sam founded the Central Appliance

Shoppers examine kitchen stoves at a Polk Bros. store, June 1954. *Wallace Kirkland/The* LIFE *Picture Collection/Shutterstock.*

and Furniture Store in 1935 at 3334 North Central Avenue. Usually known as "Polk Bros." (for the five brothers: Sol, Samuel, Morris, Harry and David), the firm grew into the largest appliance/electronics retailer in the Chicago market—and one of the biggest in the nation.

For sheer shopping fun, nothing beat a day at Polk Bros. The firm's legendary promotions included handing out 250,000 pineapples, crates of Washington apples and cases of Coca-Cola. Once, they paraded circus elephants through a store parking lot. Another time, they televised a bowling competition from inside the Polk Bros. store on Cottage Grove Avenue. For three years in the early 1960s, Polk Bros. offered molded plastic Santa Claus and snowman decorations, just five dollars with most purchases. The illuminated figures became wildly popular holiday decorations—and visible reminders of the many households that shopped at Polk Bros.

The memorable promotions drove huge foot traffic and kept the stores buzzing with action. *Hotpoint News* in 1960 stated, "Combine the evangelistic fervor of a Billy Sunday with the promotional acrobatics of a Barnum and you see why Polk Bros. moves more…appliances than any other dealer in the world."[188]

Polk Bros. moved quickly on new trends, becoming one of the first American retailers to sell color televisions and microwave ovens. It sold kitchen appliances, consumer electronics, household furniture and carpeting. At its peak in the 1950s and 1960s, Polk Bros. sold more than $100 million in appliances annually. And unlike department stores, Polk Bros. offered steep discounts and welcomed haggling with its "let's-make-a-deal" salesmen.

Over time, however, Polk Bros. had trouble fending off challenges from discount merchandisers that flooded the market. After a devastating fire at the Melrose Park headquarters in 1987 cost the company millions, the chain decided to call it quits.

NEIGHBORHOOD DEPARTMENT STORES

In addition to large specialty stores, Chicago was also home to dozens of local neighborhood general merchandise stores. Typically much smaller than the big downtown stores, they used the term *department store* rather grandly. Still, these mom-and-pop retailers often carried a surprisingly large assortment of merchandise, had good prices and benefited from their convenient neighborhood locations. Not all of them can be explored in detail here, but a few examples will give a sense of what made them beloved.

Troy Store

Rudolph Vesecky opened the first Troy store in southwest Chicago's Little Village neighborhood, then home to many Bohemian, Polish and other Eastern European residents. But his best-remembered store opened in 1938 at Cermak Road and Ridgeland Avenue in Berwyn and quickly became popular with Berwyn and Cicero residents. Historian Frank S. Magallon wrote: "In my lifetime I have heard many stories of squeaky wooden floors, basement Christmas toy displays, clothing, and other merchandise that captured the fascination of shoppers who visited the neighborhood department store. For generations of local shoppers this store was their go-to spot for everyday dry goods."[190] Like other neighborhood department stores, Troy was intimately involved in the community, sponsoring Little League teams and selling gym uniforms for local schools. It even had a shoe repair department and a beauty shop.

Troy Department Store in Berwyn, soon after closing. *David Nevers.*

Troy thrived for decades, but by the 1970s, it was struggling from changing neighborhood demographics and pressure from shopping malls. North Riverside Mall, which opened in 1975, sounded the death knell. The store was sold and eventually leveled. "Oh my gosh, the memories!!," said Phyllis Killar Janda. "Dresses for Easter and a special 'dress up' coat. There was never a question of where to go when we lived in Berwyn—we went [to] Troy store!"[191]

Gatelys Peoples Store

Another beloved—and long-lived—neighborhood department store was Gatelys Peoples Store at Michigan Avenue and 112th Street in the Roseland neighborhood. In the days when independent department stores outnumbered big urban chains, Gatelys' popularity rivaled that of Marshall Field's. It once called itself "the biggest store on Michigan Avenue."

James Gately bought the store—then named the Peoples Store—in 1917. He added his name to it, with no apostrophes, and eventually expanded it to a five-story building. Like many other neighborhood department stores, Gatelys was always a family-run business. Gately's son John opened a suburban branch store in Tinley Park in 1975.

Writer C.J. Martello collected recollections of Gatelys for *Fra Noi*: "We all remember Christmas season with Santa Claus and the windows decorated for the holidays; heading to the shoe department and stepping on the X-ray or fluoroscope machine to see the bones in your feet; or getting the same haircut every time regardless of what you wanted."[192] Readers wrote in, remembering the downstairs restaurant where you could buy a Green River soda or a full meatloaf meal for one dollar. They remembered shopping there for school uniforms: "[W]hichever school you attended, Gatelys had the right one."[193] Like many, Pete Kastanes remembered the store's doughnut machine, which plopped doughnut-shaped dough onto a conveyor belt that dropped them into sizzling oil: "It was fascinating to watch and the donuts were fresh and delicious."[194]

The store's pneumatic tube system made a memorable whooshing sound as it sent money and papers to and from the offices. James Gately himself often strolled up and down the aisles, chatting with customers and offering personal assistance. Like other neighborhood department stores, Gatelys was not a discount store but did have good prices and dependable merchandise.

The Gatelys Peoples Store hung on until 1981, when it finally shuttered, followed by the Tinley Park branch in 1994. The Roseland building stood abandoned until an extra-alarm fire in June 2019 destroyed much of it. After that, the building was demolished.

When the final Gatelys store closed, Martha Pearl McGee reminisced about shopping at Gatelys for fifty years. "I have gloves that are forty years old that I bought for $2.99, $5.99—genuine leather and pigskin, Kelly greens and mustard golds and shocking pinks and purple," she said. "I'm about to cry from seeing the store in this predicament."[195]

Rau's

One finds similar stories, involving similar beloved neighborhood department stores, from people who lived all over the greater Chicago area. For shoppers in Chicago Heights, the Rau Store at Sixteenth Street and Otto Boulevard was a landmark. Patricia O'Donnell remembered: "As grade school kids, every Christmas my sister and I would go Christmas shopping looking for a gift for our mom…and the first store we hit was Rau's….Of course we never bought anything there…it was all too expensive. But I can recall the wonderful scents of perfumes…and the gigantic merry-go-round and Santa at Christmas time…so awesome!"[196]

Rau's was purchased by Carson Pirie Scott and continued to operate as a department store, but the pull of the shopping malls eventually proved too great. Carson's closed the former Rau's location when it opened a bigger store in the massive new Lincoln Mall in nearby Matteson in 1973.

Crawford's

Another local department store, the Crawford Department Store in the West Ridge neighborhood of Chicago, took its name from the street on which the original store was located. It later opened several branches, including one in Rolling Meadows and another in Bolingbrook. The Rolling Meadows branch, opened in 1957, was the largest department store in the northwest suburbs at the time. It flourished when Rolling Meadows' population was ballooning in the 1960s and 1970s, becoming, as residents told one reporter, to Rolling Meadows what Macy's is to New York City.[197]

The original Crawford store in Chicago closed in 1981, followed by the Bolingbrook store in 1986. When the Rolling Meadows store shuttered in 1993, fans mourned. "It's easy and convenient. I can park my car right outside the store and walk in. You can't do that at Woodfield. You can't do that at Randhurst. I'm going to miss that," said customer Ken Johnson.[198]

Another shopper recalled: "I am not sure why I liked Crawford other than that it was a good old-fashioned store with Art Deco wood and glass cases and elderly clerks. For some reason I found the back entrance through the parking lot enchanting. My mom took us there frequently and she bought purses, stockings, socks and towels. I do remember that they had good deals on shoes before any of the bargain off-price shoe stores existed."[199]

South Center

Of all the neighborhood department stores, however, none had as storied— or as important—a history as South Center Department Store. Located at 421–29 East Forty-Seventh Street in the Bronzeville neighborhood for more than forty years, South Center at one point was the nation's largest Black-owned department store. The neighborhood's reputation rivaled that of 125th Street in Harlem as the nation's busiest business district for African Americans. South Center was for many years the only department store in the city that specifically served African American shoppers.[200]

Two Jewish brothers, Harry and Louis Englestein, opened South Center in 1928 in an expansive, three-story building that also housed a movie theater, a ballroom and bowling alleys.[201] The store featured a huge range of departments, including clothing, hats, jewelry, handbags, candy, shoes, toys, paint, washing machines and even canary birds. On opening day, the *Chicago Defender* predicted it would become the greatest merchandising operation on the South Side. It reported: "All during the day hundreds of people crowded the store to scrutinize the wares. With fifty different departments, everything is carried that is sold by the finest Loop stores."[202]

Even more than its size, South Center's fame came from its fair treatment of African Americans during an era of rampant discrimination by the big State Street department stores. For decades, clerks in most of the big stores routinely ignored Black customers or treated them with condescension. If African Americans could find any jobs at the big downtown department stores, they were as janitors, maids and other positions of behind-the-scenes drudgery. Most State Street department stores did not liberalize their personnel policies until the 1960s.

Postcard view of South Center Department Store, 421–29 East Forty-Seventh Street, Chicago, circa 1930.

131

In contrast, South Center broke racial barriers, hiring African Americans for all store positions from the beginning and winning over the neighborhood's predominantly Black shoppers. When it opened, the *Chicago Defender* declared that of the store's 150 employees, more than 125 were Black.[203] Years later, in 1963, the store was purchased by two African American men, John S. Sengstacke and S.B. Fuller, making it the largest Black-owned retailer in the country.

South Center operated for forty years before declaring bankruptcy and closing in 1968.

OTHER NEIGHBORHOOD DEPARTMENT STORES

There were once dozens of these neighborhood department stores spread across Chicago and its suburbs. Their names became beloved: Sabath's, Annes, Kline's, Winsberg's, Hoffing's, Lake Park, Robinson's, Siegel's, Steinberg Baum, the Globe, Colson's, Frank's, Gilmore's, Klaus, Ollswang's and many more. For most of them, little remains but a building or two and the occasional surviving matchbook. But they were an enormous part of many Chicagoans' lives. They live on in memories of squeaky wooden floors, pneumatic tubes that flew overhead and shopping for school uniforms in a store that was part of the community.

Matchbook covers advertising various Chicago neighborhood department stores: Crawford, Sabath's, Lake Park and Robinson's.

9.
CHRISTMAS ON STATE STREET

I n a masterpiece of understatement, the *Chicago Tribune* in 2017 opined, "Christmas hereabout has long meant a trip or two to State Street, which for many years was a veritable Department Store Row."[204] For most of Chicago's history, Christmas and the city's department stores went hand-in-hand.

And for obvious reasons. As the biggest season for shopping, Christmas represented the biggest season for department stores. The Chicago stores went all-out for the holidays. Little effort was needed to attract shoppers, but the stores still competed fiercely for every customer.[205]

Beginning at least as early as the 1890s, State Street would be packed with shoppers from late November through Christmas. In 1905, the *Chicago Tribune* implored department store customers to "remember what the Christmas spirit means." The crowds that year were seen surging up and down the street, "stepping upon each other and tearing each other's clothes."[206] Seven years later, in 1912, a crowd estimated at one hundred thousand people created jams so big that streetcars could move only with police assistance.[207]

Each year seemed bigger than the last. "I didn't think it was possible for any store to do such a toy business as we have done this year," said D.F. Kelly of The Fair in 1923. "Our toy business was thirty to forty percent over last year's and last year was an unprecedented year in this store." Other merchants thought Kelly too conservative. To encourage shoppers to make their purchases early, some business associations began staging toy parades and other festivities prior to Thanksgiving. It would help with the crowds—and the bottom line. "If Thanksgiving could be moved back to the first Thursday in November it would be the biggest thing imaginable for the toy trade," said the buyer for Marshall Field's toys in 1928.[208]

By the 1930s and 1940s, as many as a million shoppers jammed into the Loop's retail corridor on the busiest holiday shopping days. Merchants urged shoppers to avoid the busiest hours. One advertisement implored, for "convenience, comfort, leisurely selection, and the best of service—use the early forenoon hours."[209] By the 1970s, the State Street Council was supplying free bus service to and from various train stations and city parking garages, as well as guidebooks on how to catch the right CTA bus or subway to return home.[210]

Thousands came just to walk down State Street, marveling at the animated window displays in the department store windows. The tradition of elaborately decorated windows in December was already firmly established by the 1920s, but in that era, these were not narrative stories. The windows instead brimmed with gift ideas, especially toy displays. Every year, Marshall Field's reserved its large corner window at State and Washington Streets for a spectacular display of toys.

By World War II, non-narrative vignettes had become popular. In 1943, the Marshall Field's windows showed a variety of staged scenes of American homes, with well-dressed mannequins returning to their cottages, townhomes, farmhouses and suburban homes.

For Marshall Field's, the year 1944 marked a change. That year, the windows told a complete narrative story, using Clement Clarke Moore's classic poem, "A Visit from St. Nicholas." As viewers walked from one Field's window to the next, they could read each successive verse and see its accompanying scene. It was such a hit that Field's simply repeated the same windows the next year.

Unfortunately for Field's, other stores quickly followed suit, creating their own "Visit from St. Nicholas" narrative holiday windows. Field's executives realized the store needed its own proprietary holiday character.[211] So in 1946, the Marshall Field's windows introduced Chicagoans to a jolly character named Uncle Mistletoe. Invented by window-display designer Johanna Osborne, Uncle Mistletoe wore a bright red overcoat and a black top hat with a sprig of mistletoe. His role, as Santa's ambassador-at-large, was to travel the world searching for children remembering to take time to be kind at Christmas. He was joined in 1948 by his wife, Aunt Holly.

An estimated half-million parents and children jammed State Street to cheer the arrival of Santa Claus, November 19, 1949. *Bettmann/Getty Images.*

Uncle Mistletoe grew so popular that by the late 1940s and early 1950s, he was starring in his own television show and presiding over the store's Kindness Club. Over the years, new characters joined the lineup, including Freddie Fieldmouse and his wife, Marsha, in the 1970s. A white teddy bear named Mistletoe Bear appeared in 1986.

Popular as he was, Uncle Mistletoe was not the first department store Christmas character in Chicago. Pre-dating him was Montgomery Ward's wildly popular character, Rudolph the Red-Nosed Reindeer. Rudolph was born as a result of Ward's search for an inexpensive holiday giveaway. For years, Montgomery Ward had been giving out free children's coloring books (bought from local vendors) as holiday promotions. But in 1939, a store executive reasoned the company could save money if it created something in-house instead. A young advertising copywriter named Robert L. May was assigned to come up with a children's Christmas story as that year's giveaway. Inspired by Chicago's wintry fog and his daughter's love of zoo animals, he wrote an inspirational poem about an outcast reindeer that

Christmas shoppers admire window displays on State Street, December 1933. *DN-A-4841/* Chicago Sun-Times/Chicago Daily News *Collection/Chicago History Museum.*

saves Christmas.[212] "Rudolph the Red-Nosed Reindeer" was an instant hit. By the time Gene Autry recorded a hit song about Rudolph in 1949, rights had been transferred from the store to May.[213]

Wieboldt's had the Cinnamon Bear, a holiday character that originated in Portland, Oregon. In 1937, Portland husband-and-wife team Glanville and

A window from Marshall Field's 1944 "A Visit from St. Nicholas" display. That year marked the first time Field's used its Christmas windows to tell a narrative story. *HB-08288-B, Chicago History Museum, Hedrich-Blessing Collection.*

Elisabeth Heisch wrote a twenty-six-episode radio show about a brother and sister who team up with a bear named Paddy O'Cinnamon to retrieve their Christmas tree's missing silver star. Portland department store Lipman-Wolfe and Company initially sponsored the show for the Portland market, but over time, numerous department stores around the country picked it up.[214] In the 1940s and 1950s (and again briefly in the mid-1980s), Wieboldt's sponsored annual radio broadcasts of *The Cinnamon Bear* for the Chicago area, airing six times a week between Thanksgiving and Christmas. "I so remember when at Christmas time they would have the *Cinnamon Bear* radio show and coloring contest. I would sit by the radio and listen to every word of every program," said one anonymous Wieboldt's fan on a department store history website.[215] The store also staged appearances by Paddy O'Cinnamon, gave out themed coloring books, sponsored a television version of the show and sold Cinnamon Bear stuffed animals. Ruth Lawler remembered: "Such fond memories. We used to come down [to Wieboldt's on State Street] at Christmas, then we'd stop for corned beef and coffee at a Jewish deli near the Chicago Theatre. The children used to listen to 'The Cinnamon Bear.'"

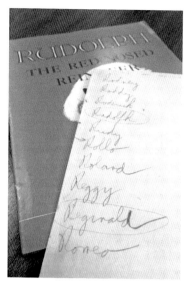 

Left: Rudolph the Red-Nosed Reindeer could have been named Rollo or Reginald instead, as this handwritten list of possible names shows. The list is now part of a special collection at Dartmouth College from the estate of Robert May, a Dartmouth graduate who wrote the famous story in 1939 for Montgomery Ward. *Toby Tablot/AP/Shutterstock.*

Right: Besides Rudolph the Red-Nosed Reindeer, other popular Chicago department store Christmas characters included the Cinnamon Bear (Wieboldt's) and Uncle Mistletoe (Marshall Field's).

One time my daughter put her Cinnamon Bear in the corner mailbox and my husband had to wait for the postman to get it out."[216]

Not all department store holiday characters took off. Goldblatt's Timmy the Gingerbread boy in the 1970s fizzled. Carson Pirie Scott had a Martian Bear (the 1974 theme was Christmas in Outer Space), but it soon disappeared.

Holiday characters that succeeded, however, became merchandise bonanzas. Marshall Field's offered a huge variety of Uncle Mistletoe and Aunt Holly products, including stuffed dolls, ceramic cookie jars, molded candles, vinyl records, ornaments, coloring books and even a Little Golden Book.

Most stores created their Christmas window displays in-house, writing charming rhyming verses to accompany each vignette that parents could read aloud. The Carson Pirie Scott windows in 1948 told *The Tale of Meow*, featuring a mischievous kitten that shows up in Santa's workshop. A typical verse read

'Twas a cat small and furry
Who made a quick bow,
Then softly he whispered
A stately "Meow."[217]

The Carson Pirie Scott building's distinctive two-story corner entrance provided an ideal display space for holiday tableaux to accompany its holiday windows. A serene nativity scene appeared there in 1952, when Carson's used the story of *Amahl and the Night Visitors* (a recent television opera based on the biblical story of the Three Kings) as the theme for its Christmas window displays. When the Carson's windows told the story of *A Christmas Carol*, the entry displayed a giant Bob Cratchit with Tiny Tim perched on his shoulder. And when Carson's windows featured the story of *The Nutcracker*, an enormous nutcracker went up, towering over State Street.

Hundreds of Chicago families made an annual tradition of walking from one end of State Street to the other, viewing each store's window displays. In 1965, if you walked from Randolph to Congress Street, you would have seen Uncle Mistletoe and Aunt Holly starring in the Marshall Field's windows and the story of the birth of Jesus in the Carson's windows. Wieboldt's

Children examine a Christmas window display at the Wieboldt's store on State Street, December 1975. *ST-200035020011-0003/*Chicago Sun-Times *collection/Chicago History Museum.*

showcased capering "Wee Folk." Montgomery Ward featured a children's dream forest. Goldblatt's windows starred a seal named Frostiseal, and Santa Claus himself took the lead in the Sears windows.[218]

It is difficult to date precisely when department stores in Chicago began offering visits with Santa Claus, although photographs showing children visiting with Santa in the stores exist as early as the 1910s. Certainly, it was a well-established tradition by the 1930s. The Fair in 1950 offered six photos with Santa for one dollar (chatting with him in his in-store gingerbread house was free).[219]

Santa's home at Carson Pirie Scott was the stage of the store's eighth-floor auditorium, adjacent to the Heather House. In a typical Christmas season in the 1970s, as many as two thousand children a day might visit Santa at Carson's.[220] At Marshall Field's, he could be found in Cozy Cloud Cottage, in the furniture section on the eighth floor. For most of the year, this small model home was called the Trend House and was used to display interior-decorating trends. At Christmas, the entire structure would be transformed into a decorated home for Santa. Visitors standing in line to see Santa Claus would wind through several festively decorated rooms while waiting.

By midcentury, Chicago's holiday season even commenced near the department stores, with the crowning of a Queen of State Street. Chosen by the State Street Council, her duties included lighting the State Street's Christmas decorations and starring in the Christmas parade.

The State Street Christmas parade began in 1934 as a way to stimulate shopping during the Great Depression. It soon became the annual, and much beloved, kick-off celebration for the Christmas shopping season in Chicago. Even in particularly frosty years, spectators turned out, wrapping themselves in blankets and sitting on curbs padded with newspapers. High school marching bands frequently appeared in the parade, as did floats and balloon inflatables. The 1948 parade included eleven giant balloons, one of them a sixty-foot Noah's Ark, with animals' heads bobbing in the windows.[221] Part of the fun every year was catching celebrities, such as Bozo the Clown, star of the hit children's television show *Bozo's Circus*. "What a parade this is," grumbled one six-year-old in 1965 after Chicago mayor Richard J. Daley and radio personality Sigmund "Sig" Sakowitz had passed. "I've been here hours and I haven't seen a celebrity yet."[222]

With the postwar baby boom, department store holiday activities continued to grow. At The Fair, children could take a ride on an indoor train for five cents. Christmas window displays grew bigger, and so did the

Christmas decorations can be seen over the entrance at Carson Pirie Scott in this photograph of the corner of State and Madison Streets, taken on a warm, foggy day, circa 1968. *Kim Vintage Stock/Alamy.*

budgets. Christmas windows accounted for 60 percent of most department stores' annual window budgets by midcentury.[223]

No store, however, did it bigger than Marshall Field's. During the holiday season, Field's main aisle featured dazzling decorations, often soaring into the north and south light wells. On the fourth floor, giant candy canes transformed the toy section into Candy Cane Lane. The Walnut Room for many years featured a forty-eight-foot-tall fresh evergreen tree. Field's employees would travel north to Minnesota or Michigan each fall to select the perfect tree. The ideal tree's top fifty feet or so would be shipped by railroad to Chicago. After the store closed on a Saturday night, the tree

Above: The State Street Council's Christmas parade passes Wieboldt's and Carson Pirie Scott on November 28, 1965. *ST-30004551-0013*, Chicago Sun-Times *collection, Chicago History Museum.*

Right: A Christmas advertisement for The Fair, *Chicago Tribune*, December 11, 1949, plugs kiddie train rides for five cents and pictures with Santa for six for a dollar.

The great Christmas tree in the Walnut Room at Marshall Field's, 1956. *Frank Scherschel/The LIFE Picture Collection/Shutterstock.*

would be carried in through the Randolph Street doors (their revolving doors having been temporarily removed) and hoisted up the north light well. In the Walnut Room, workers could heave the tree into position atop the drained fountain. Until the store switched to an artificial tree in the early 1960s, a team of firefighters stood guard twenty-four hours a day.

Field's also offered an annual choral concert in the Walnut Room. The Marshall Field's Choral Society, launched in 1907, consisted of about two hundred employees. In addition to their annual Christmas performance, they also gave a concert every May in Orchestra Hall.

Field's executives emphasized that its festivities were the company's gift to the city. While true, the goal was also to make the big store a destination. By successfully associating itself with the holiday season, Field's cemented its reputation as the leading retail institution in Chicago. The Marshall Field's animated windows became an eagerly anticipated tradition, but what they really sold was the store's institutional leadership.

For employees of the big department stores, what made the holiday decorations special was their handmade quality. Sallie Posniak spent forty-one years at Marshall Field's, helping to design and create the five thousand or so ornaments made annually for the Walnut Room tree. Planning began as soon as the current year's tree was up. After a theme was chosen, research

Marshall Field's State Street store decorated for Christmas, 1977. *ST-16001908-0010,* Chicago Sun-Times *collection/Chicago History Museum.*

and design took about four months. Production began in May and lasted for six months. Once the tree itself was in place, three-story-tall scaffolding went up around it, and crew members worked for about forty-eight hours to hang all the decorations.

To make the soaring tree look even taller, ornaments ranged in size. The smallest, just five or six inches in diameter, hung at the top, while the biggest eighteen-inch ornaments hung on the bottom limbs. It was, Posniak explained, "a labor of love, the ornaments made by hand."[224]

The popularity of the department-store holiday traditions transcended their commercial underpinnings. Families made an annual tradition of visits to see the State Street windows and anticipated them eagerly. Dining in the Walnut Room at Christmas became such a tradition that it continues to this day. "I started going with my mother and my sister when I was five and I'm eighty-two now," said shopper Bonnie Pollack. "We got there when they opened, and we had it timed." To ensure they'd get a good spot in line, she revealed, "we always were last in the elevator, so we'd get off first."[225]

Christmas at Marshall Field's grew so substantial that even Chicagoans who rarely shopped there came to see the Christmas displays. "It was such a big deal to me," Mary Michalik recalled for the *Los Angeles Times* about her annual visit with her six siblings. "We didn't really buy anything—maybe a cookie at the bakery—but my mom made us feel that we were so lucky....We were going to the ritziest store in the world."[226]

EPILOGUE

Of the seven department stores on State Street in 1947, all of them are gone. First, they closed their State Street stores. Then, they disappeared forever.

The death came slowly, starting with an exodus of Chicago residents from the city after World War II. A mix of white flight and economic disinvestment caused foot traffic on State Street to decline. As suburban stores cannibalized their customers, the big stores began to deteriorate. Discount stores proliferated on State Street, strip clubs and adult bookstores began popping up and some theaters switched to exploitation films.

In 1979, a mile-long stretch of State Street was transformed into a car-free zone in an effort to revitalize the Loop shopping district. The city spent $17 million to widen the sidewalks, install sculptures and plant trees. The State Street Mall opened to great fanfare in 1979.[227]

It flopped. Rather than drawing lively crowds, the mall's jumbo sidewalks gave the area an empty, desolate feel. Diesel fumes from the buses filled the air. The thoroughfare converted back to automobile traffic in 1996.[228]

How much the mall contributed to the decline of State Street's department stores is hard to gauge given the forces already in play by 1979. Still, it did not help. Multiple big stores on State Street closed in the 1980s: Goldblatt's (1981), Sears (1983), Montgomery Ward (1985), Lytton's (1986), Wieboldt's (1987) and Chas. A. Stevens (1989).

But even the end of the mall could not stop the thoroughfare's decline. Carson Pirie Scott closed its flagship State Street store in 2006, the same year that all Marshall Field's stores were converted to Macy's.

Thousands of Chicagoans attended noontime festivities dedicating the new State Street Mall, October 29, 1979. *Larry Stoddard/AP/Shutterstock.*

A Chicago-area Montgomery Ward store announces "Total Liquidation" as going-out-of-business sales began in January 2001. *Stephen J. Carrera/AP/Shutterstock.*

Customers packed the closing sale at the Six Corners Sears, the last remaining Sears store in the city of Chicago, on May 13, 2018. *Patrick Gorski/NurPhoto via Getty Images.*

Some Chicago department stores continued to operate their smaller stores in outlying locations, but gradually those too closed. Montgomery Ward filed for bankruptcy in 1997 and closed its remaining stores in 2001. (The brand was acquired by a catalog marketer, which relaunched Montgomery Ward as an online retailer in 2004.) In 2018, the last remaining local department stores, Carson Pirie Scott (under its parent company Bon-Ton) and Sears filed for bankruptcy and closed virtually all their stores.

What happened? Analysts point to some familiar culprits: the proliferation of discount chain stores, the rise of off-price clothing retailers, internet shopping and the decline of the middle class.[229] In most cases, multiple issues played a role. A devastating fire ravaged Polk Bros. headquarters in 1992. That, combined with the poor economy and stiff competition, caused executives to close the business.[230]

None of these struggles was unique to Chicago. By the turn of the millennium, department stores nationwide had begun to feel like remnants of a previous era. By the 2010s, their closings felt belated. General retailers no longer seemed to have a place in the competitive world of online shopping, discount giants and fast fashion. An analysis by the *Washington Post* found that roughly 40 percent of the nation's department stores closed

Demolition work began in 2019 on the vacant Carson Pirie Scott store in Matteson, Illinois, which had been one of the anchors of Lincoln Mall. *Mike Nolan*/Daily Southtown/Chicago Tribune *Archive Photos/TCA.*

between 2016 and 2021. Many more were predicted to close by the end of the decade.[231]

Still, the closures broke many hearts. Stevens president John W. Lee II found the closing of Chas. A Stevens "a lot like losing a loved one."[232] Former Field's employee Becky Petropoulos said, "I remember them taking the Marshall Field's sign off the side of the building and putting the Macy's sign up while we were all outside watching, and it was pretty tragic."[233]

Others mourn the strong retail communities that vibrant department stores could support. "The old Sears in downtown Waukegan, once a magical place where J.C. Higgins bikes and baseball gloves, along with Ted Williams fishing tackle, introduced kids of all ages to the outdoors, vanished decades ago," wrote Charles Selle in 2018. "When it left, a large part of Waukegan's downtown retail base went with it."[234]

They might be gone, but these stores left behind indelible memories. Customers remember the role they played in everyday life, as in this anonymous reply to an online article about Goldblatt's: "My wife and I made our first major purchase, a sewing machine, at the Goldblatt's on Twenty-sixth Street in Little Village. We paid for it on lay-away and made payments every week with a coupon book until the machine was paid off. We still have the machine forty-two years later."[235] During Chas. A. Stevens' liquidation sale in 1989, customer Jane Cahill said, "I've been shopping here since high school and that's about twenty years. My mother got her wedding dress here."[236]

Linda Scheffer of Hebron, Indiana, remembered when the Carson's store near her opened. "My mother had muscular dystrophy and the mall was her haven of mobility, especially in the winter. We shopped at Carson's from the beginning," she said. Scheffer's family progressed from buying swimwear and school clothes there to prom dresses and, later, baby clothes for grandchildren. "When I lost my mother in October 2015, it was Carson's I went to to feel her presence. I broke down one afternoon in the purse department shortly after she passed. A saleswoman walked up and just held me as I cried. My sister and I joke that the closing of Carson's had to have something to do with my mom no longer shopping there. It's a lifetime of memories. Sweet memories."[237]

Another former Field's employee, Julie Blake, put it this way: "My allegiance to Marshall Field's wasn't because I worked there, it was because I was almost raised in the store. Probably from the time I was five or six until I was a teenager, every Saturday, my mother, my sister and I would take two buses and an L down to Marshall Field's, put our coats in a locker, get a stroller and spend the entire day in the store. I mean it was such a special place."[238]

Home-grown department stores, which used local rather than centralized merchandising, made a difference in customers' loyalties. "The buyers at Field's understood the market the way others didn't," said customer Valerie Nicholson. "Field's got it right....You'd shop there for your prom dress, for your birthday, for white gloves to ride on the train downtown."[239]

The loss of Marshall Field's hit Chicagoans especially hard. For many decades, buying something from Field's signified the good life. It became the epitome of destination shopping. As historian David Garrard Lowe put it: "It's one of the real Chicago institutions. People came from all over. Field's was more than a store to a lot of people."[240]

Marshall Field's closure has bred, as the *New York Times* put it, a new kind of superfan.[241] Fans take photos of themselves in front of the bronze plaques still bearing the store's name. "It's hard to imagine any other retailer commanding such fierce loyalty that customers are compelled to photograph the corporate logo."[242] Chicagoans still meet under the great clocks and flock to State Street during the holidays to eat in the Walnut Room. They buy green mugs and sweatshirts with the Marshall Field's logo.

Chicago's State Street is no longer a crowded canyon of block-long department stores where you can buy anything from a paper clip to a $10,000 oil painting. You can no longer drop in on seven of the world's biggest stores, walk the longest sales aisle in the world or wander a dreamworld of Parisian gowns, gold-inlaid chess sets and 1,478 varieties of salt shakers, as you could in 1955.[243]

Still, the past resonates strongly up and down State Street. Chicagoans with long memories can see remnants of this past glory as they wander the street. Carson Pirie Scott's glorious flagship store building sat vacant for five years before being converted into the Sullivan Center, a mixed-use space with retail space for a Target Store on the lower floors and office and academic space on the upper floors. Sears' former flagship store at State and Van Buren Streets is now home to Robert Morris University. Goldblatt's former flagship on State Street now houses part of DePaul University's downtown campus. Sharp-eyed pedestrians can even spot the terra-cotta *R*s in the building's façade, honoring the Rothschild's store.

The former Carson Pirie Scott store at 1 South State Street in 2014, after its conversion to the Sullivan Center. *Steve Geer/iStock.*

The former Goldblatt's building on State Street is now the DePaul Center, part of DePaul University's Loop campus. *DePaul University Buildings Collection/Special Collections and Archives/ DePaul University Library.*

Many other retailer-built structures also remain. The Sears Tower, now Willis Tower, still stands, as does the Merchandise Mart, now theMART, which houses manufacturers' showrooms and stylish offices. Montgomery Ward's catalog house, where workers once dashed around on roller skates to fetch merchandise, was redeveloped in the early 2000s into residences and an expansive office building. A number of former Wieboldt's stores stood empty for years before being remodeled to become other stores (Yorktown Center, Harlem Irving Plaza), converted to lofts and other commercial uses (Lincoln/Ashland/Belmont) or just demolished (River Forest, Evanston). Other department-store buildings in outlying locations have followed a similar pattern, being converted to use as stores, condominiums, retirement communities, lofts and even, in one case, a school.

Nearly a thousand Sears kit houses remain in the area, especially in Elgin, Aurora, Joliet and Downers Grove.[244] Old catalogs are treasured, not only as collectors' items but also as a useful record of the customs and habits of middle-class Americans of the past. Even the names of Chicago's great merchants live on. Both Robert E. Wood (Sears) and Marshall Field survive in the name of Woodfield Mall in Schaumburg.

Marshall Field's clock at State and Washington Streets. *Greg McAfee Photography/Shutterstock.*

The north light well at Macy's on State Street (formerly Marshall Field's), 2015. *Rupert Oberhauser/imageBROKER/Shutterstock.*

We still benefit from the philanthropy of Chicago's merchants. Gifts from Chicago's department-store magnates helped support numerous cultural institutions, including the Museum of Science and Industry (Julius Rosenwald), the Shedd Aquarium (John Shedd) and the Field Museum (Marshall Field). The city's lakefront parks owe much to retailer Montgomery Ward, who fought so long to keep that land open. The Wieboldt Foundation and Polk Bros. Foundation are among the Chicago area's largest charitable organizations.

The one flagship building on State Street that still operates as a department store is the former Marshall Field's building, now known as "Macy's on State Street." The great corner clocks remain, as do the columns lining the main aisle, the magnificent light wells, the Tiffany mosaic and an annual Christmas tree in the Walnut Room.

More importantly than all of this, we have their legacy. Chicago's department stores showed an uncanny ability to anticipate important changes in the marketplace. Marshall Field's, Carson Pirie Scott and The Fair pioneered the kind of large, full-line department stores made possible by new technological advances in transportation, communications and architecture. Montgomery Ward and Sears perfected mail order when America was still mostly rural and then pivoted to brick-and-mortar stores with the rise of the automobile. Goldblatt's and Wieboldt's discovered that a department-store chain could secure a major slice of the department-store market even without a presence in the central downtown.

If department stores symbolize a city's spirit and personality, Chicago's stores reveal this city as an epicenter of energy, innovation and deep civic pride.

NOTES

Introduction

1. Philip Hampson, "World Famous State St. Vital to Chicago Life," *Chicago Tribune*, June 10, 1947.
2. "State Street Emerges from Mire and Becomes the Greatest Retail Trade Center in the World," *Chicago Tribune*, July 1, 1956.
3. Hampson, "World Famous," *Chicago Tribune*.
4. "The Department Store in the West," *Arena* 22 (September 1897): 320.
5. Jan Whitaker, *Service and Style: How the American Department Store Fashioned the Middle Class* (New York: St. Martin's Press, 2006), 12–13.
6. Hampson, "World Famous," *Chicago Tribune*.
7. Whitaker, *Service and Style*, 14–15.
8. Editorial, *Chicago Tribune*, January 28, 1881.
9. Whitaker, *Service and Style*, 79.
10. "The Marshall Field Story," *Chicago Tribune*, February 10, 1952.
11. "Department Store in the West," *Arena*, 320.
12. Daniel A. Graff, "Retail Workers," Encyclopedia of Chicago (website), accessed October 24, 2021, http://www.encyclopedia.chicagohistory.org.
13. Joel A. Tarr, "The Chicago Anti-Department Store Crusade of 1897: A Case Study in Urban Commercial Development," *Journal of the Illinois State Historical Society* 64, no. 2 (1971): 161–72, http://www.jstor.org/stable/40190914.

14. Richard Longstreth, "Bringing 'Downtown' to the Neighborhoods: Wieboldt's Goldblatt's, and the Creation of Department Store Chains in Chicago," *Buildings & Landscapes: Journal of the Vernacular Architecture Forum,* 14 (Fall 2007), 13–49.

15. "Marshall Field, the Store," *Fortune* (December 1945): 142–47.

16. Whitaker, *Service and Style,* 292.

17. "Fall College Fashions," *Life,* August 26, 1946, 107–8, 111.

18. Whitaker, *Service and Style,* 27.

Chapter 1

19. "Field's Starts Celebration of 100th Birthday," *Chicago Tribune,* January 11, 1952. See also Eleanor Page, "Field's Store Is Honored on Its Centennial," *Chicago Tribune,* January 11, 1952.

20. Joseph Egelhof, "Big Volume of Book Business," *Chicago Tribune,* October 24, 1952.

21. "Dry Goods," *Chicago Tribune,* October 13, 1868.

22. "Under the Clock: Marshall Field's Sets the Times," *Chicago Tribune Magazine,* November 8, 1992.

23. Lloyd Wendt and Herman Kogan, *Give the Lady What She Wants* (Chicago: Rand McNally, 1952), 223.

24. Nancy F. Koehn, *Brand New: How Entrepreneurs Earned Consumers' Trust from Wedgwood to Dell* (Boston: Harvard Business School Press, 2001), 119.

25. Wendt and Kogan, *Give the Lady,* 213.

26. Ibid., 235–36.

27. Robert Spector, *The Legend of Frango Chocolate* (Kirkland, WA: Documentary Book Publishers, 1993), 6–12.

28. Marshall Field and Co., *Marshall Field and Company Chicago* (Chicago: 1951).

29. James Iska, "My City of Memory," *Chicago Stories,* James Iska (website), accessed January 24, 2017, http://jamesiska.com.

30. Wendt and Kogan, *Give the Lady,* 376.

31. Kate Wells, "Marshall Field's Stylish," *Reminisce* (April/May 2007): 22–23.

32. Larry Bennett, "Shopping Districts and Malls," Encyclopedia of Chicago (website), accessed March 11, 2019, http://www.encyclopedia.chicagohistory.org.

33. Carol Zetek Goddard, in discussion with the author, September 8, 2010.

34. Michael Lisicky, "Racial Injustice Outlives the American Department Store," *Forbes*, June 6, 2020, https://www.forbes.com.

35. Curious City team, "A Different Perspective on Our Story About the Walnut Room," *Curious City*, WBEZ Chicago, December 22, 2020, https://www.wbez.org.

36. Jerry Knight, "Batus Inc. to Acquire Field Stores," *Washington Post*, March 17, 1982, https://www.washingtonpost.com.

37. Neil Steinberg, "25 Years On, the Soggy Story of the Loop Flood Lingers," *Chicago Sun-Times*, April 7, 2017.

38. David Matthews, "Marshall Field's Lives on at Macy's, 10 Years after the Big Name Change," *DNAInfo*, September 8, 2016, https://www.dnainfo.com.

39. Danny Miller, "State Street Sweet: Frango Mints Aren't Native, but Their Spirit Is Pure Chicago," *Saveur* (October 2007): 16.

Chapter 2

40. Les Raff, "Carsons Department Stores Are Closing for Good, and I Care. Do You?" ChicagoNow, April 19, 2019, https://www.chicagonow.com.

41. John Vinci, "Carson Pirie Scott: 125 Years in Business," *Chicago History* 8, no. 2 (Summer 1979): 92.

42. Frances MacKinnon, "Amboy to Get Plaque from Carson Pirie Scott," *Dixon (IL) Evening Telegraph*, October 30, 1975.

43. "Carson Pirie Scott & Company History," FundingUniverse, accessed March 29, 2020, http://www.fundinguniverse.com.

44. "Story of Growth Carson Pirie, Scott & Co. During 80 Years, Told by Journal," *Dixon (IL) Evening Telegraph*, August 3, 1934.

45. Joseph M. Siry, *Carson Pirie Scott: Louis Sullivan and the Chicago Department Store* (Chicago: University of Chicago Press, 1988), 188.

46. Wendy Bright, "The Story of Louis Sullivan's Carson Pirie Scott Store," August 14, 2018, WendyCity, accessed March 29 2020, http://wendycitychicago.com.

47. Blair Kamin, "Missed Opportunity," *Chicago Tribune*, April 24, 1994.

48. "Big Store Is Sold," *Chicago Tribune*, August 12, 1904.

49. Gayle Soucek, *Carson's: The History of a Chicago Shopping Landmark* (Charleston, SC: The History Press, 2013), 106.

50. Advertisement, *Cap and Gown* 10 (University of Chicago, 1905): 362.

51. Advertisement, *Chicago Tribune*, March 30, 1925.

52. Fred Farrar, "State St. Will Always Command Its Share of Market: Martin," *Chicago Tribune*, December 2, 1962.

53. Ernest Fuller, "State St.: It's Still Biggest 'Shop Center,'" *Chicago Tribune*, July 23, 1955.

54. "Feast Opens O'Hare's New Luxury Dining Complex," *Chicago Tribune*, March 26, 1963.

55. Menu, Heather House Restaurant, Carson Pirie Scott, November 22, 1969, *Chuckman's Chicago Nostalgia*, https://chuckmanchicagonostalgia. wordpress.com.

56. Lynn Taylor, "Many Retailers Open on Sunday, Watch Results," *Chicago Tribune*, November 16, 1969.

57. Michael Edgerton, "He Knows How to Sell," *Chicago Tribune*, July 4, 1977.

58. Richard Klicki, "Bankruptcy Sale Marks End of Carson's," *Daily Herald* (Arlington Heights, IL), April 19, 2018, https://www.dailyherald.com.

59. Raff, "Carsons Department Stores."

60. Joseph Sjostrom, "Carsons Unveils Rotunda," *Chicago Tribune*, August 15, 1979.

61. Greg Jones, April 19, 2018, comment on "Bankruptcy Sales Marks End of Carson's," *Daily Herald* (Chicago), https://www.dailyherald.com.

62. Joseph F. Pete, "All Region Carson's to Close Forever on Wednesday," *Times of Northwest Indiana* (Munster, IN), August 26, 2018, https://www. nwitimes.com.

63. Lauren Rohr, "'I Hate to See It Go': Shoppers Reminisce at Carson's on Its Last Day," *Daily Herald* (Arlington Heights, IL), August 29, 2018, https://www.dailyherald.com.

64. Rohr, "'I Hate to See It Go,'" *Daily Herald*.

65. Pete, "All Region Carson's to Close," *Times of Northwest Indiana*.

Chapter 3

66. Theodore Dreiser, *Sister Carrie* (1900; repr. New York: Penguin, 1994), 22.

67. Forrest Crissey, *Since Forty Years Ago: An Account of the Origin and Growth of Chicago and Its First Department Store* (Chicago: The Fair, 1915).

68. Whitaker, *Service and Style*, 32–33.

69. "Chicago Now Has the Largest Store in the World," *Inter Ocean* (Chicago, IL), September 12, 1897.

70. Crissey, *Since Forty Years*.

71. Ibid.

72. "Death of E.J. Lehmann," *Chicago Tribune*, January 7, 1900, 6.

Chapter 4

73. U.S. Bureau of the Census, *Historical Statistics of the United States, Colonial Times to 1970, Bicentennial Edition, Part 1* (Washington, DC: 1975), 12.

74. Cecil C. Hoge Sr., *The First Hundred Years Are the Toughest: What We Can Learn from the Century of Competition Between Sears and Wards* (Berkeley, CA: Ten Speed Press 1988), 10.

75. Ibid., 16.

76. "Store Closing: Montgomery Ward," transcript, *PBS NewsHour*, PBS, February 5, 2001, https://www.pbs.org.

77. "The Most Influential Businessmen," *Forbes*, July 28, 2005, https://www.forbes.com.

78. Hoge, *First Hundred Years*, 17.

79. Frank B. Latham, *1872–1972 A Century of Serving Consumers: The Story of Montgomery Ward* (Chicago: Montgomery Ward, 1972), 14.

80. *Montgomery Ward Catalogue and Buyers Guide of 1895*, facsimile edition (Garden City, NY: Dover Publications, 1969).

81. Latham, *1872–1972*, 45.

82. Ibid., 47.

83. "Death Takes Ward, Lake 'Watchdog,' Following Fall," *Chicago Tribune*, December 8, 1913.

84. Latham, *1872–1972*, 45.

85. "Store Closing: Montgomery Ward," *PBS NewsHour*.

86. *Fortune*, January 1935.

87. Latham, *1872–1972*, 81.

88. "Montgomery Ward: Prosperity Is Still Around the Corner," *Fortune*, November 1960.

89. ABC News, "Montgomery Ward Shuts Its Doors," ABC News, December 28, 2000, https://abcnews.go.com.

90. "Store Closing: Montgomery Ward," *PBS NewsHour*.

91. "Wards Files for Ch. 11," CNNMoney, December 28, 2000, https://money.cnn.com.

92. "Store Closing: Montgomery Ward," *PBS NewsHour*.

Chapter 5

93. Louis Goldblatt, *Life Is a Game, Play to Win!* (N.p.: Lindenhouse Books, 1995), 83–84.

94. "Trace History of Goldblatt Department Stores' Growth," *Daily Herald* (Arlington Heights, IL), April 5, 1962, 197.

95. "Ibid.

96. Goldblatt, *Life Is a Game*, 82.

97. Ibid., 129–30.

98. "Trace History," *Daily Herald.*

99. Goldblatt, *Life Is a Game*, 145.

100. Longstreth, "Bringing 'Downtown,'" 23.

101. "Chicago Welcomes Opening of Rothschild and Co.'s New Store; Some New Features of the Monument to Trade; Mr. Rosenthal of Ft. Wayne Interested," *Fort Wayne (IN) Journal-Gazette*, October 20, 1912.

102. Wendt and Kogan, *Give the Lady*, 298–99.

103. "JG Industries, Inc." FundingUniverse, accessed May 21, 2020, http://www.fundinguniverse.com.

104. Advertisement, *Chicago Tribune*, July 5, 1936.

105. StrayKitten, December 3, 2010, comment on "Goldblatt's," Forgotten Chicago Forum, https://forgottenchicago.com.

106. Goldblatt, *Life Is a Game*, 168.

107. Kenan Heise, "Maurice Goldblatt, 92; Cofounded Store," *Chicago Tribune*, July 18, 1984.

108. Longstreth, "Bringing 'Downtown,'" 36.

109. "Goldblatt Opening Set," *Daily Herald* (Arlington Heights, IL), April 5, 1962.

110. Goldblatt, *Life Is a Game*, 145.

111. Philip Hampson, "Views Chicago as Showcase of the World," *Chicago Tribune*, September 3, 1954.

112. Janet Key, "Goldblatt's: Bravado to Bankruptcy," *Chicago Tribune*, December 27, 1981.

113. Longstreth, "Bringing 'Downtown,'" 13–49.

114. Shirleywalker, March 10, 2015, comment on "Goldblatt's," Forgotten Chicago Forum, https://forgottenchicago.com.

Chapter 6

115. Lloyd Wendt, "State Street Chicago," *Rotarian* (March 1955): 25.

116. "Chicago's Newest Shopping Palace," *Inter Ocean* (Chicago, IL), September 24, 1912.

117. "Mandel Brothers Joins Boycott of Nazi Goods," *Jewish Daily Bulletin*, April 4, 1934, Jewish Telegraphic Agency Archive, https://www.jta.org.

118. "Shoppers Pack Stores in Great Buying Spree," *Chicago Tribune*, November 29, 1952.
119. "Mandel Brothers," Jazz Age Chicago (website), accessed January 4, 2021, https://jazzagechicago.wordpress.com.
120. "Merger to Put Wieboldt's on State Street," *Chicago Tribune*, April 23, 1960.
121. Ibid.
122. Whitaker, *Service and Style*, 46–47.
123. Letter of William Wieboldt to his parents, October 30, 1871, The Great Chicago Fire and the Web of Memory (website), Chicago History Museum, accessed September 5, 2020, https://www.greatchicagofire.org.
124. "Mrs. Wieboldt Is Dead at 102; Store Founder," *Chicago Tribune*, February 25, 1958.
125. "W.A. Wieboldt Company," Jazz Age Chicago (website), accessed September 22, 2020, https://jazzagechicago.wordpress.com.
126. "Wm. Wieboldt Rites Planned for Tomorrow," *Chicago Tribune*, December 11, 1954.
127. Elmer F. Wieboldt, *People Policies Profits: A Contribution to Wieboldt's Continued Progress* (n.p.: Wieboldt Stores, 1944), 6–7.
128. "Wm. Wieboldt Rites," *Chicago Tribune*.
129. Longstreth, "Bringing 'Downtown,'" 18.
130. "W.A. Wieboldt," Jazz Age Chicago.
131. Al Chase "Wieboldt Buys Rosenberg Co. in Evanston," *Chicago Tribune*, September 15, 1929.
132. "Wieboldt's Will Begin Stamp Program," *Chicago Tribune*, October 16, 1957.
133. Wieboldt, *People Policies Profits*, 11.
134. Pete Kastanes, "My Memories of Wieboldt's Department Store in Chicago," *Vanished Chicagoland Stories* (blog), July 28, 2019, https://vanishedchicagoland.blog
135. Advertisement, *Chicago Sun-Times*, March 13, 1983.
136. Jill Bettner, "Stamp Saving Becoming Unstuck," *Daily Herald* (Arlington Heights, IL), March 20, 1976.
137. Janet Key, "Wieboldt to Shut State Street Store," *Chicago Tribune*, June 10, 1987.
138. Betsy Weiss Van Die, "Windy City Memories…of the Way Department Stores Were," *Consumer Grouch* (blog), October 4, 2011, http://www.consumergrouch.com.

Chapter 7

139. Advertisement, *Chicago Tribune*, February 1, 1925.

140. "Chronology of the Sears Catalog," Sears Archives, accessed February 25, 2021, http://www.searsarchives.com.

141. "Sears, Roebuck and Co. History," FundingUniverse, accessed February 7, 2021, http://www.fundinguniverse.com.

142. Lorin Sorensen, *Sears, Roebuck and Co.: 100th Anniversary 1886–1986* (St. Helena, CA: Silverado Publishing, 1985), 23.

143. "Sears Homes 1933–1940," Sears Archives, accessed August 23, 2021, http://www.searsarchives.com.

144. Darcel Rockett, "Cataloging History: A Nostalgic Look at Chicago's Sears Kit Homes Still Standing Throughout Chicagoland," *Chicago Tribune*, November 28, 2018.

145. Sorensen, *Sears, Roebuck*, 45–46.

146. Richard Longstreth, "Sears, Roebuck and the Remaking of the Department Store, 1924–42," *Journal of the Society of Architectural Historians* 125, no 2 (June 2006): 241.

147. Daniel Raff and Peter Temin, "Sears Roebuck in the Twentieth Century: Competition, Complementaries, and the Problem of Wasting Assets," *NBER Working Papers Series on Historical Factors in Long Run Growth* (Cambridge, MA: National Bureau of Economic Research, 1997), 13.

148. "Sears History—1925," Sears Archives, accessed February 25, 2021, http://www.searsarchives.com.

149. Sorensen, *Sears, Roebuck*, 68.

150. Longstreth, "Sears, Roebuck," 245, 251.

151. Sorensen, *Sears, Roebuck*, 70–71.

152. Donald L. Miller, *City of the Century: The Epic of Chicago and the Making of America* (New York: Simon & Schuster, 1996), 347.

153. "Store History—Chicago, Illinois," Sears Archives, accessed February 25, 2021, http://www.searsarchives.com.

154. Amanda Garrity, "The Sears Wish Book Changed the Way America Does Christmas," *Good Housekeeping*, December 20, 2019, https://www.goodhousekeeping.com.

155. Al Chase, "Chicago to Have World's First Windowless Department Store," *Chicago Sunday Tribune*, May 20, 1934.

156. "Store History—Chicago: Irving Park Store," Sears Archives, accessed February 25, 2021, http://www.searsarchives.com.

157. Sorensen, *Sears, Roebuck*, 95.

158. Ibid., 107.

159. Ibid., 106.

160. Lauren Zumbach, "Chicago's Last Sears Store to Close for Good Sunday," *Chicago Tribune*, July 15, 2018.

161. Lara I. Lord, comment on "Are you sad to see many Sears stores closing?" December 25, 2019, Quora, https://www.quora.com.

162. Tricia McKinnon, "The Downfall of Sears, 5 Reasons Why It's Struggling to Survive," *Indigo Digital* (blog), July 10, 2020, https://www.indigo9digital.com.

163. John S. DeMott, "Sears' Sizzling New Vitality," *Time*, August 20, 1984, 83.

164. Traci Parker, "Sears' Complicated History with Black Customers," *Baltimore Sun*, May 10, 2019, https://www.baltimoresun.com.

165. Vicki Howard, "The Rise and Fall of Sears," *Zócalo Public Square*, SmithsonianMag, July 25, 2017, https://www.smithsonianmag.com.

166. Sean Scallon, comment on Rod Dreher, "Remember Sears?," *American Conservative*, May 1, 2012, https://www.theamericanconservative.com.

167. Stephanie Strom, "Sears Eliminating Its Catalogues and 50,000 Jobs," *New York Times*, January 26, 1993.

168. Rod Dreher, "Remember Sears?," *American Conservative*, April 29, 2012, https://www.theamericanconservative.com.

169. Les Mikesell, comment on "Why do people not visit Sears that often anymore?," September 24, 2018, Quora, https://www.quora.com.

170. Eric Bronsky, "The Roebuck Stops Here," February 20, 2016, The Trolley Dodger (website), https://thetrolleydodger.com.

171. Steve Corbyn, comment on "Do Americans not like to shop at Sears and why?," May 20, 2020, Quora, https://www.quora.com.

172. Val Perry Rendel, *Sears in Chicago: A Century of Memories* (Charleston, SC: The History Press, 2019), 14, 158.

Chapter 8

173. "17 Stories Height of Boston Store," *Chicago Tribune*, August 22, 1991. See also Margaret Corwin, "Mollie Netcher Newbury: The Merchant Princess," *Chicago History* 6, no. 1 (Spring 1977): 34–43.

174. Miller, *City of the Century*, 260.

175. "End of a Legend," *Time*, July 29, 1946, http://content.time.com.

176. Advertisement, *Inter Ocean* (Chicago), September 24, 1893.

177. "Chicago Welcomes Opening," *Fort Wayne (IN) Journal-Gazette*.

178. Janet Key, "Investor Group Buys Charles A. Stevens," *Chicago Tribune*, February 28, 1986.

179. Janet Key, "Chas. A. Stevens Files for Chapter 11," *Chicago Tribune*, June 23, 1988.

180. "Baby Boomers Remember: Shopping in Old La Grange," *Patch* (La Grange, IL), April 25, 2011, https://patch.com/Illinois/lagrange/baby-boomers-remember-shopping-in-old-la-grange.

181. Goody, "Defunct Department Stores-Chas A. Stevens," *Eat the Blog* (blog), February 25, 2014, https://eattheblog.blogspot.com/2014/02/defunct-department-stores-chas-stevens.html.

182. "Lytton, Pioneer State Street Merchant in Chicago, Dies at 102," *Decatur (IL) Daily Review*, March 31, 1949.

183. Robert P. Ledermann, *Christmas on State Street: 1940s and Beyond* (Charleston SC: Arcadia Publishing, 2002), 25.

184. "Lytton, Pioneer," *Decatur Daily Review*.

185. Edward Wilson, "Henry C. Lytton, Founder of 'Hub,' Is 100 Saturday," *Chicago Tribune*, July 10, 1947.

186. "New Bramson Store to Open in Park Forest," *Chicago Tribune*, July 15, 1958.

187. Jorge Casuso, "Sol Polk, Co-Founder of Polk Bros. Stores," *Chicago Tribune*, May 16, 1988.

188. Ann Paden, "Polk's Promotion Machine," *Chicago Tribune*, January 19, 1997.

189. "Our Story," Polk Bros. Foundation (website), accessed August 1, 2021, www.polkbrosfdn.org.

190. Frank S. Magallon, "If you are sitting back and reminiscing about Berwyn or Cicero with any long time or past resident over the age of 45 or so, the subject of Berwyn's Troy Store always comes up!," The Old Berwyn Cicero Chicago History Page, Facebook, January 20, 2014, www.facebook.com.

191. Phyllis Killar Janda, comment on Magallon, "If you are sitting back," Facebook, January 20, 2014, www.facebook.com.

192. C.J. Martello, "Stirring up Memories of Gatelys Peoples Store," *Fra Noi*, February 17, 2016, https://franoi.com.

193. Ibid.

194. Pete Kastanes, "My Memories of Gatelys Peoples Store in Roseland," *Vanished Chicagoland* (blog), June 2, 2019, https://vanishedchicagoland.blog.

195. Mark Caro, "All Sales Will Be Final for Gatelys and Its Era," *Chicago Tribune*, October 13, 1994.

196. Patricia O'Donnell, comment on Historic Chicago Heights, "One hundred years ago THE RAU STORE was a retailing institution to the shoppers of Chicago Heights," Facebook, November 20, 2020, https://www.facebook.com.

197. Joseph Kirby, "Town Not Buying Crawford's Closing," *Chicago Tribune*, February 4, 1993.

198. Ibid.

199. Weiss Van Die, "Windy City Memories," *Consumer Grouch*.

200. Erick Johnson, "The Black Department Store on King Drive," *Chicago Crusader*, February 23, 2018, https://chicagocrusader.com.

201. "Huge Cinema and Ballroom at 47th-Grand," *Chicago Tribune*, August 29, 1926.

202. "South Center," Jazz Age Chicago (website), accessed March 24, 2021, https://jazzagechicago.wordpress.com.

203. Ibid.

Chapter 9

204. Ron Grossman, "State Street Magic," in *Chicago Flashback: The People and Events That Shaped a City's History* (Evanston, IL: Agate Midway, 2017), 356.

205. Whitaker, *Service and Style*, 118.

206. "Christmas Shopping," *Chicago Tribune*, November 23, 1905.

207. "Shopping Crowd Jams Loop: Biggest Throng in Holiday History Blocks Traffic," *Chicago Tribune*, December 22, 1912.

208. C.W. Butterworth, "The Holidays in Chicago," *Playthings* (December 1928): 276.

209. Advertisement, *Chicago Tribune*, December 14, 1928.

210. Wayne Dunham, "Yuletide Pastimes: A Wealth of Low-Cost Cheer," *Chicago Tribune*, December 8, 1973.

211. Whitaker, *Service and Style*, 119.

212. Robert L. May, "Robert May Tells How Rudolph, The Red-Nosed Reindeer, Came into Being," *Gettysburg (PA) Times*, December 22, 1975, https://news.google.com.

213. Jessica Pupovac, "Writing 'Rudolph': The Original Red-Nosed Manuscript," (transcript), *Morning Edition*, NPR, December 25, 2013, https://www.npr.org.

214. "The Cinnamon Bear and Paddy O'Cinnamon," PdxHistory (website), accessed December 16, 2020, http://www.pdxhistory.com.

215. Anonymous, November 15, 2016, comment on "Wieboldt's Chicago, Illinois," The Department Store Museum (website), http://www.thedepartmentstoremuseum.org.

216. "'Everything Must Go'—and Does," *Chicago Tribune*, July 19, 1987.

217. Advertisement, *Chicago Tribune*, November 27, 1948.

218. "State Street's Most Colorful Christmas," *Chicago Tribune*, December 8, 1965.

219. Advertisement, *Chicago Tribune*, December 17, 1950.

220. Sean Toolan, "Can't Keep Santa on Farm," *Chicago Tribune*, November 30, 1975.

221. Grossman, "State Street Magic."

222. "The Old Santa," *Chicago Tribune*, November 30, 1965.

223. Whitaker, *Service and Style*, 118.

224. Victoria Scott, "Trimming the Marshall Field's Tree," *Evanston (IL) RoundTable*, December 14, 2016, https://evanstonroundtable.com.

225. Bonnie Pollack, in discussion with the author, December 14, 2020.

226. Bonnie Miller Rubin, "Chicagoans Flock to Marshall Field's For Memories," *Los Angeles Times*, December 26, 2005, https://www.latimes.com.

Epilogue

227. Mary Wisniewski, "Chicago Flashback: Failure and Bus Fumes," *Chicago Tribune*, October 27, 2019.

228. Dirk Johnson, "Chicago Gives a Pedestrian Mall the Boot," *New York Times*, February 1, 1996.

229. Jason Del Rey, "The Death of the Department Store and the American Middle Class," *Vox*, November 30, 2020, https://www.vox.com.

230. Jason Schmeltzer, "End of an Era: Polk Bros. to Close Doors," *Chicago Tribune*, April 3, 1992.

231. Abha Bhattarai, "Mall Department Stores Were Struggling. The Pandemic Has Pushed Them to the Edge of Extinction," *Washington Post*, April 16, 2021, https://www.washingtonpost.com.

232. Lisa Holton, "Shoppers Say Goodbye to Old Friend—Chas. A. Stevens Begins Liquidation Sale," *Chicago Sun-Times*, February 15, 1989.

233. Daphne Howland, "Macy's Windy City Blues," Retail Dive, March 1, 2021, https://www.retaildive.com.

234. Charles Selle, "Carson's Joins the Roll Call of Failing Retail Brands," opinion, *Lake County (IL) News-Sun*, April 30, 2018.

235. Chitransplant, August 4, 2014, comment on "Goldblatt's," Forgotten Chicago Forum, https://forgottenchicago.com.

236. Holton, "Shoppers Say Goodbye."

237. Pete, "All Region Carson's to Close," *Times of Northwest Indiana*.

238. Howland, "Macy's Windy City Blues."

239. Tim Cronin, "Former Shopping Landmark to Be Demolished," *Daily Southtown* (Chicago, IL), October 26, 2010.

240. Andrew Harris, "Chicago Still Miffed at Macy's," *Seattle Times*, September 11, 2007, https://www.seattletimes.com.

241. Libby Sander, "Loss of a Beloved Department Store Breeds a New Kind of Superfan," *New York Times*, January 17, 2007, https://www.nytimes.com.

242. Rubin, "Chicagoans Flock," *Los Angeles Times*.

243. Wendt, "State Street Chicago," 24.

244. "Why Does Chicago Have So Few Sears Homes?" Sears Homes of Chicagoland (website), February 4, 2020, http://www.sears-homes.com.

INDEX

A

African Americans 12, 132
  as department store customers 34,
    51, 111
  as department store employees 33,
    53, 111
Aldens 13
Amboy, IL 39
anti-department-store protests 12
anti-mail-order protests 64
Avery, Sewell 68, 70, 106
"A Visit from St. Nicholas" 134

B

Back of the Yards (neighborhood) 76
Barr, John A. 70
BATUS 35
Becker-Ryan 106
Berwyn, IL 128
Bon Marché 57
Bon-Ton 54, 149
Boston Store, the 57, 116–118
  clock 11
  State Street building 113, 117
Bramson 124, 125
Brickyard 17
Bronzeville (neighborhood) 12, 131
Brooker, Robert E. 70
Burnham, Daniel 10, 42

C

Carson Pirie Scott 155
  bankruptcy 149
  brides 15
  choir 13
  Christmas 140
  Christmas windows 138, 139
  college board 16, 125
  Corporate Level 53
  County Seat 54
  Heather House 48–51
  Martian Bear 138
  memories 55, 151
  Seven Continents restaurant 48
  State Street entrance 43, 53
  State Street store 11, 44, 147
  State Street store restaurants 48–53
Carson, Samuel 39
Century of Progress 14, 106
Chas. A. Stevens 120–122, 125, 147,
    150, 151
  1912 building 122
  memories 122
  State Street store 122
Chicago Mail-Order Company 13
Chicago Ridge (shopping mall) 113
Christmas parade 16, 140
Christmas windows 94, 109, 129, 140,
    145

Cinnamon Bear 138
Cloud Room 33
Colchester, IL 120
college boards 16, 124–125
Container Corporation of America 70
Conway, MA 21
County Seat 54
Cozy Cloud Cottage 140
Crawford (department store) 130, 132

D

Davis Store 78, 79, 119
Dayton-Hudson 35, 36
DePaul University 85, 152–153
discount stores 16, 73, 96, 108, 111,
    127, 147, 149
display windows 13, 23, 27–28, 106,
    119, 122
Dixie Square 70
Dziennik Chicagoski 92

E

Edens Plaza 46–47
Englestein, Harry and Louis 131
Englewood (neighborhood) 93, 96, 106
ethnic/immigrant customers 12, 51,
    57, 76, 90
Evanston, IL 27, 35, 93, 94, 98, 153
Evergreen Plaza 46, 51, 70, 124

F

Fair, the 70, 155
    1897 building 10, 58–60
    early store 9, 57–58
    food service 23
    Randhurst store 60, 70
    toys 133
    train ride 140, 142
fashion shows 19, 32, 51, 124
Federated Department Stores 37
Field, Joseph 22
Field, Leiter and Co. 10, 22

Field, Marshall 7, 10, 19, 21, 23, 87, 155
    death 24
Field, Palmer and Leiter 21, 62
Ford City 17, 96
Frango chocolates 29, 30, 38
Fraser, Arthur 27
Frederick and Nelson 27, 35

G

Gary, IN 33, 78
Gately, James 129
Gatelys Peoples Store 129
General Electric 73
Give the Lady What She Wants 22, 30
G. Linning 92
Goldblatt, Hannah 74
Goldblatt, Joel 74, 75, 79, 84
Goldblatt, Louis 74, 75, 77, 79, 81
Goldblatt, Maurice 74, 75, 79
Goldblatt, Nathan 75
Goldblatt's 155
    closure 85
    early stores 12
    memories 79, 86, 150–151
    State Street store 14, 79, 85, 147,
        152–153
    Timmy the Gingerbread Boy 138
Goldblatt, Simon 74
Golf Mill 108, 110, 124
Graham, Anderson, Probst & White 92
Grange (Patrons of Husbandry) 62, 63
Great Chicago Fire 9, 22, 40, 63, 87, 90

H

Halle's 35
Hammond, IN 48, 78
Harlem Irving Plaza 94, 95, 153
H.C. Struve 76
Heather House 48–51
H.G. Selfridge (department store) 44
Hillside (shopping center) 16, 46
Houston, TX 35
Hub, the. See Lytton's

I

Iverson (store) 75

J

J.B. Ivey 35
Jenney, William Le Baron 9, 105
Joliet, IL 78

K

Kelly, D.F. 133
Klein, Simon 87
Kresge, S.S. 59–60

L

Lake Forest, IL 27
Lake Street shopping district 7, 20
Lampert, Edward 113
Larkin Company 76
Larson, Glenn I. 51
Lederer 76
Lee, John W., II 150
Lehmann, Ernst J. 9, 56–59
Leiter, Levi 7, 9, 21, 118
Lincoln Mall 130, 150
Lincoln Village 89
Lytton, Henry C. 123–124
Lytton's 120, 122–125, 147

M

MacLeish, Andrew 40
Macy's 37, 57, 58, 147, 150
Mandel Bros. 7, 10, 87–89
  1912 building 88
Mandel, Solomon 87
Marcor 70, 72
Marshall Field's
  28 Shop 29–30
  1902 building 10, 24
  1907 building 10, 24
  1914 expansion 10, 19, 27
  1992 flood 36
  books 19
  brides 15
  Budget Floor 23
  chicken pot pie 23, 31
  choir 13, 144
  Christmas tree 141–145
  Christmas windows 134–135, 137,
    139, 144
  clocks 11, 24, 36, 37, 152, 155
  Cloud Room 33
  conversion to Macy's 37, 147, 150
  Davis Store 78, 79, 119
  early restaurants 23
  fashion shows 31, 32
  Fashions of the Hour 27
  Frango chocolates 27–29, 38
  Freddie and Marsha Fieldmouse 135
  manufacturing 27
  memories 151, 152
  Mistletoe Bear 135
  State Street store restaurants 23, 27
  Store for Men 27, 30, 35
  Tiffany mosaic 11, 25, 38, 155
  toys 19, 30, 33, 134, 141
  Trend House 30, 140
  Uncle Mistletoe and Aunt Holly
    134–135, 138, 139
  Walnut Room 19, 31, 141, 143, 144,
    145, 152, 155
  wholesale 27
  window displays 27, 134–135, 137,
    139
Martin, C. Virgil 48
Matteson, IL 130, 150
Maurice L. Rothschild 119, 124, 125
May Department Stores 37
Mayer, David 40
May, Robert L. 135–136
Merchandise Mart 27, 153
Michigan Avenue shopping district 17,
  34
Mobil Oil 72
Montgomery Ward
  after 2004 149
  and The Fair 60, 70

bankruptcy 149
catalog 12, 62–66, 70, 73, 155
Chicago Avenue plant 66, 153
competition with Sears 65, 72
first catalog 63
first stores 67
kit houses 66
memories 73
Michigan Avenue headquarters 65, 72
State Street store 70, 71, 147
Superior St headquarters 72
Morris, Nelson 9, 119

N

Neighborhood department stores
    127–132
Netcher, Charles 116
Netcher, Mollie 116–118
North Riverside (shopping mall) 114,
    128

O

Oak Brook, IL 34
Oak Park/River Forest shopping
    district 16, 27, 35, 60, 70, 94,
    124, 153
O'Hare Airport 48
Old Orchard 16, 70, 124
Osborne, Johanna 134

P

P.A. Bergner 54
Palmer House 9
Palmer, Potter 9, 20, 21
parcel post 65, 100
Pardridge (dry goods store) 116
Park Forest Plaza 16, 34, 46, 81, 124
Pearl Harbor 14
Pirie, John T. 39
Polk Bros. 120, 125–127
  closure 127, 149
  foundation 127, 155
Polk, Sol 125, 127

P. Palmer Dry Goods 7, 20
Price, Vincent 109

Q

Queen of State Street 140

R

Randhurst 60
Rau Store 130
Robert Morris University 152
Roebuck, Alvah C. 99
Rolling Meadows, IL 130
Roseland (neighborhood) 129
Rosenberg's 93
Rosenwald, Julius 101, 102, 155
Rothschild, Abram M. 9, 119
Rothschild, Maurice L. 119, 124
Rothschild's 119, 152
Rudolph the Red-Nosed Reindeer
    135–136, 138
rural free delivery 64, 65, 100

S

Santa Claus, visits with 129, 130, 140,
    142
Schlesinger and Mayer 10, 11, 44–45
Scott, George and Robert 40
Scottsdale shopping center 81
Sears 155
  bankruptcy 113
  catalog 12, 65, 99, 99–102, 102, 106,
    111
  Christmas catalog 106, 109
  competition with Montgomery Ward
    65–67, 72, 108
  first store 99, 102, 110
  Hoffman Estates headquarters 111
  Homan Avenue headquarters
    100–101
  kit houses 102, 153
  memories 109, 113, 115
  merger with Kmart 113
  monorail ride 109

post-World War II expansion 106, 108, 109
racial and gender inequalities at 111, 112
rivalry with Montgomery Ward 108
State Street store 14, 105, 113, 147, 152
towers 101, 104, 109, 153
WLS (radio) 104
Sears, Richard 12, 65, 100, 101
Second Leiter Building 9, 10, 104–105, 118
Selfridge, Harry Gordon 23
Chicago store 44–45, 45
Selfridge's (department store) 44
Shedd, John G. 24, 27, 155
S&H Green Stamps 94–96
shopping malls/shopping centers 16, 34, 46, 70, 81, 120, 122
Siegel, Cooper 10, 105, 118
Since Forty Years Ago 57, 59
Sister Carrie 56
Six Corners shopping district 106, 109, 113, 149
Skokie, IL 34
South Center Department Store 131–132
Spiegel 13
State Street Council 16, 48, 98, 134, 140
State Street Mall 147
State Street shopping district 7–9, 17, 48, 58
racial discrimination 131
Stevens Charles Anthony 120
Sullivan Center 152
Sullivan, Louis 11, 42–44

T

Telling, Edward 110
Thorne, George 63
Tinley Park, IL 129
Tobin, James 90
Trend House 30, 140

Troy (department store) 128
28 Shop 30

V

Vesecky, Rudolph 128

W

Wanamaker's 33
Ward, Aaron Montgomery 12, 61–66, 155
death 66
Water Tower Place 17, 34
Waukegan, IL 33, 150
Wauwatosa, WI 34
West Ridge (neighborhoood) 130
Wieboldt, Anna Louisa Kruger 90, 92
Wieboldt, Elmer 92, 96
Wieboldt Foundation 92, 98, 155
Wieboldt's 125, 155
acquisition of Mandel Bros. 89
Cinnamon Bear 137–138
closure of State Street store 98, 147
early resemblance to downtown stores 77, 94
early stores 12, 90–92
memories 96, 98
S&H Green Stamps 94–96, 98
State Street store 87, 94, 96–98
Toyteria 98
Wieboldt, Werner 92
Wieboldt, William A. 90–92
WLS. *See* Sears
Woodfield Mall 16, 17, 113, 153
Wood, Robert E. 66, 102, 103
World's Columbian Exposition 23, 42, 65, 118

Y

Yamasaki, Minoru 72
Yorktown (shopping center) 70, 153

ABOUT THE AUTHOR

Karen Kring.

L eslie Goddard is an award-winning historian who has been writing and lecturing about topics in American history and women's history for more than twenty years. She holds a PhD in interdisciplinary studies and an MA in museum studies and is the author of several books on Chicago history, including *Remembering Marshall Field's* (Arcadia Publishing, 2011) and *Chicago's Sweet Candy History* (Arcadia Publishing, 2012). Audiences in more than thirty states have enjoyed her history presentations, including at the Chicago Public Library, Illinois Humanities Council, Chicago History Museum, Art Institute of Chicago, Road Scholars, Victorian Society in America, Questers International and hundreds of libraries, colleges, clubs, civic organizations and Chautauqua festivals. A former museum director, she is a lifelong resident of the Chicago area. In addition to her own brief stint as a Marshall Field's sales associate, Leslie's extended family has more than seventy years' collective experience working for Chicago department stores.